OUT & ABOUT

• WALKING GUIDES TO BRITAIN •

No 3

The Midlands

To

Catherine

Happy Birthday

lots of Love

Robert ×

10-4-97

MARSHALL CAVENDISH

First published in Great Britain in 1995 by
Marshall Cavendish Books, London
(a division of Marshall Cavendish Partworks Ltd)

Copyright © 1995 Marshall Cavendish

ISBN 03190 057 55

British Library Cataloguing in Publication Data:
A catalogue record for this book is available from the British Library

Printed and bound in Dubai, U.A.E.

Some of this material has previously appeared in the Marshall Cavendish partwork OUT & ABOUT

CONTENTS

Introduction to

OUT & ABOUT

• WALKING GUIDES TO BRITAIN •

Walking has become one of the most popular pastimes in Britain. To enjoy walking, you don't need any special skills, you don't have to follow rules or join expensive clubs, and you don't need any special equipment – though a pair of walking boots is a good idea! It is an easy way of relaxing and getting some exercise, and of enjoying nature and the changing seasons.

The OUT & ABOUT WALKING GUIDES TO BRITAIN will give you ideas for walks in your own neighbourhood and in other areas of Britain. All the walks are devised around a theme and range in length from about 2 to 9 miles (3.25 to 14.5 km) and in difficulty from very easy to mildly strenuous. Since each walk is circular, you will always be able to get back to your starting point.

Devised by experts and tested for accuracy, all the walks are accompanied by clear, practical instructions and an enlarged section of the relevant Ordnance Survey map. The flavour of the walk and highlights to look out for are described in the introductory text.

LOCAL COLOUR

Background features give you extra insight into items of local interest. The OUT & ABOUT WALKING GUIDES TO BRITAIN relate legends, point out unusual architectural details, provide a potted history of the lives of famous writers and artists connected with a particular place, explain traditional crafts still practised by local artisans, and uncover the secrets behind an ever-changing landscape.

DISCOVER NATURE

One of the greatest pleasures in going for a walk is the sense of being close to nature. On the walks suggested in the OUT & ABOUT WALKING GUIDES TO BRITAIN, you can feel the wind, smell the pine trees, hear the birds and see the beauty of the countryside. You will become more aware of the seasons – the life cycles of butterflies, the mating calls of birds, the protective behaviour of all creatures with their young. You will see the beginning of new life in the forests and fields, the bluebell carpets in spring woodlands, the dazzling beauty of rhododendron bushes in early summer, the swaying cornfields of summer and the golden colours of leaves in autumn. The OUT & ABOUT WALKING GUIDES TO BRITAIN tell you what to look out for and where to find it.

NATURE WALK

Occasional nature walk panels. will highlight an interesting feature that you will see on your walk. You will learn about natural and manmade details in the landscape, how to tell which animal or bird has nibbled the cones in a pine forest, what nurse trees are and what a triangulation point is.

FACT FILE

The fact file will give you at-a-glance information about each walk to help you make your selection.

⊛ **general location**

os **map reference for Ordnance Survey map with grid reference for starting point**

miles 0 1 2 3 4 5 6 7 8 9
kms 0 1 2 3 4 5 6 7 8 9 10 11 12 13 14 15 **length of the walk in miles and kilometres**

◑ **time needed if walking at an average speed**

▬ **character of the walk: easy/easy with**

◼ **strenuous parts/mildly strenuous; hills to**

▲ **be climbed and muddy or dangerous areas are pointed out**

P **parking facilities near the start of the walk**

T **public transport information**

▤ **facilities for refreshment, including pubs**

🍴 **serving lunchtime meals, restaurants, tea rooms and picnic areas**

WC **location of toilets**

⨇ **historic sites**

ORDNANCE SURVEY MAPS

All the walks in the OUT & ABOUT WALKING GUIDES TO BRITAIN are illustrated on large-scale, full-colour maps supplied by the Ordnance Survey. Ordnance Survey are justifiably proud of their worldwide reputation for excellence and accuracy. For extra clarity, the maps have been enlarged to a scale of 1:21,120 (3 inches to 1 mile).

The route for each walk is marked clearly on the map with a broken red line, and the numbers along the

ABOVE: *Colourful narrowboats are always an attractive feature on inland waterways.*

route refer you to the numbered stages in the written directions. In addition, points of interest are marked on the maps with letters. Each one is mentioned in the walk directions and is described in detail in the introductory text.

COUNTRYWISE

The countryside is one of our greatest resources. If we treat it with respect, we can preserve it for the future.

Throughout the countryside there is a network of paths and byways. Some are former trading routes, others are simply the paths villagers took to visit one another in the days before public transport. Most are designated 'rights of way': foot-paths, open only to people on foot, and bridleways, open to people on foot, horseback or bicycle. These paths can be identified on Ordnance Survey maps and verified, in cases of dispute, by the definitive map for the area, held by the relevant local authority.

THE LAW OF TRESPASS

If you find a public right of way barred to you, you may remove the obstruction or take a short detour around it. However, in England and Wales, if you stray from the footpath you are trespassing and could be sued in a civil court for damages. In Scotland, rights of way are not recorded on definitive maps, nor is there a law of trespass. Although you may cross mountain and moorland paths, landowners are permitted to impose restrictions on access, such as during the grouse-shooting season, which should be obeyed.

If you are following a public right of way and find, for example, that your path is blocked by a field of crops, you are entitled to walk the line of the footpath through the crops, in single file. Farmers are required, by law, to restore public rights of way within 14 days of ploughing. However, if you feel uncomfortable about doing this and can find a way round, then do so. But report the matter to the local authority who will take the necessary action to clear the correct route.

RIGHT: *The stunning patchwork of fields surrounding the picturesque village of Widecombe in the heart of Dartmoor makes a beautiful setting for the famous annual fair.*
BELOW: *Brown hares boxing in spring are a fascinating sight.*

It is illegal for farmers to place a bull on its own in a field crossed by a right of way (unless the bull is not a recognized dairy breed). If you come across a bull alone in a field, find another way round.

COMMONS AND PARKS

There are certain areas in England and Wales where you may be able to wander without keeping to paths, such as most commons and beaches. There are also country parks, set up by local authorities for public recreation – parkland, woodland, heath or farmland.

The National Trust is the largest private landowner in England and Wales. Its purpose is to preserve areas of natural beauty and sites of historic interest by acquisition, holding them in trust for public access and enjoyment. Information on access may be obtained from National Trust headquarters at

THE COUNTRY CODE

■ **Enjoy the countryside, and respect its life and work**

■ **Always guard against risk of fire**

■ **Fasten all gates**

■ **Keep your dogs under close control**

■ **Keep to public footpaths across farmland**

■ **Use gates and stiles to cross fences, hedges and walls**

■ **Leave livestock, crops and machinery alone**

■ **Take your litter home**

■ **Help to keep all water clean**

■ **Protect wildlife, plants and trees**

■ **Take special care on country roads**

■ **Make no unnecessary noise**

36 QueenAnne's Gate, London SW1H 9AS
Tel: 071-222 9251.

ABOVE RIGHT *Carelessness with cigarettes, matches or camp fires can be devastating in a forest.*

Most regions of great scenic beauty in England and Wales are designated National Parks or Areas of Outstanding Natural Beauty (AONB). In Scotland, they are known as National Scenic Areas (NSAs) or AONBs.

Most of this land is privately owned and there is no right of public access. In some cases, local authorities may have negotiated agreements with landowners to allow walkers access on mountains and moors.

CONSERVATION

National park, AONB or NSA status is intended to provide some measure of protection for the land-scape, guarding against unsuitable development while encouraging enjoyment of its natural beauty.

Nature reserves are areas set aside for conservation. Most are privately owned, some by large organizations such as the Royal Society for the Protection of Birds. Although some offer public access, most require permission to enter.

THE RAMBLERS ASSOCIATION

The aims of the Ramblers Association are to further greater understanding and care of the countryside, to protect and enhance public rights of way and areas of natural beauty, to improve public access to the countryside, and to encourage more people to take up rambling as a healthy, recreational activity. It has played an important role in preserving and developing our national footpath network.

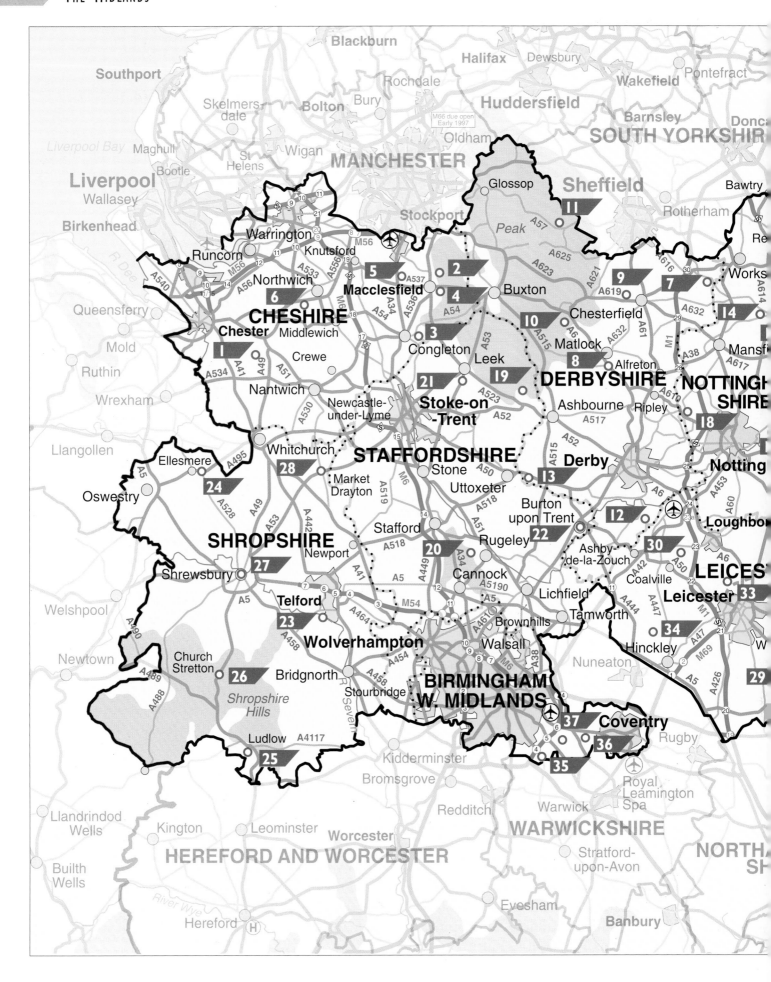

The Midlands

All the walks featured in this book are plotted and numbered on the regional map (left) and listed in the box below.

1 At the Base of the Pennines
2 The Cloud and the Bridestones
3 Tegg's Nose Summit
4 On the Edge
5 The Salt Mines and the Abbey
6 Creswell Crags
7 The Cromford Canal
8 The Linacre Valley
9 Lathkill Dale
10 Along Derwent Edge
11 Two Halls and an Abbey
12 Hall and Bridges
13 Sherwood Forest
14 Along the River Trent
15 The Fields of Laxton
16 Hilltop and Towpath
17 Lawrence Country
18 The Manifold Valley
19 A Medieval Hunting Ground
20 Mill and Kilns
21 Going for a Burton
22 Ironbridge Gorge
23 Shropshire's Lake District
24 A Perfect Historic Town
25 The Long Mynd
26 By Dogpole and Grope Lane
27 Finding the Four Alls
28 Along the Towpath
29 Bradgate Park
30 Burrough Hill
31 A Walk on the Water
32 Mount St Bernard Abbey
33 Bosworth Field
34 Forest of Arden Heathlands
35 The Heart of England
36 At England's Centre

USING MAPS

Although the OUT & ABOUT WALKING GUIDES TO BRITAIN give you all the information you need, it is useful to have some basic map skills. Most of us have some experience of using a motoring atlas to navigate by car. Navigating when walking is much the same, except that mistakes are much more time and energy consuming and, if circumstances conspire, could lead to an accident.

A large-scale map is the answer to identifying where you are. Britain is fortunate in having the best mapping agency in the world, the Ordnance Survey, which produces high-quality maps, the most popular being the 1:50,000 Landranger series. However, the most useful for walkers are the 1:25,000 Pathfinder, Explorer and Outdoor Leisure maps.

THE LIE OF THE LAND

A map provides more than just a bird's eye view of the land; it also conveys information about the terrain – whether marshy, forested, covered with tussocky grass or boulders; it distinguishes between footpaths and bridleways; and shows boundaries such as parish and county boundaries.

Symbols are used to identify a variety of land-marks such as churches, camp and caravan sites, bus, coach and rail stations, castles, caves and historic houses. Perhaps most importantly of all, the shape of the land is indicated by contour lines. Each line represents land at a specific height so it is possible to read the gradient from the spacing of the lines (the closer the spacing, the steeper the hill).

GRID REFERENCES

All Ordnance Survey maps are over-printed with a framework of squares known as the National Grid. This is a reference system which, by breaking the country down into squares, allows you to pinpoint any place in the country and give it a unique reference number; very useful when making rendezvous arrange-ments. On OS Landranger, Pathfinder and Outdoor Leisure maps it is possible to give a reference to an accuarcy of 100 metres. Grid squares on these maps cover an area of 1 km x 1 km on the ground.

GIVING A GRID REFERENCE

Blenheim Palace in Oxfordshire has a grid reference of **SP 441 161**. This is constructed as follows:

SP These letters identify the 100 km grid square in which Blenheim Palace lies. These squares form the basis of the National Grid. Information on the

100 km square covering a particular map is always given in the map key.

441 161 This six figure reference locates the position of Blenheim Palace to 100 metres in the 100 km grid square.

44 This part of the reference is the number of the grid line which forms the western (left-hand) boundary of the 1 km grid square in which Blenheim Palace appears. This number is printed in the top and bottom margins of the relevant OS map (Pathfinder 1092 in this case).

16 This part of the reference is the number of the grid line which forms the southern (lower) boundary of the 1 km grid square in which Blenheim Palace appears. This number is printed in the left- and right-hand margins of the relevant OS map (Pathfinder 1092).

These two numbers together (SP 4416) locate the bottom left-hand corner of

the 1 km grid square in which Blenheim Palace appears. The remaining figures in the reference **441 161** pinpoint the position within that square by dividing its western boundary lines into tenths and estimating on which imaginary tenths line Blenheim Palace lies.

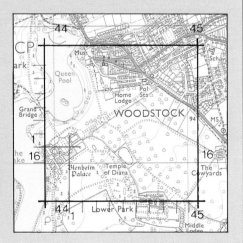

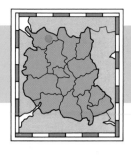

way along the hills, is 18½ miles (30 km) long. It runs along the gritstone escarpment from Lyme Hall in the north to Rushton in the south.

The Macclesfield Canal **D** was fully operational in 1831 and is 27³/₄ miles (45 km) long with 13

◄ *The town of Bollington, on the edge of the Pennines, seen from the vantage point of White Nancy. Growing by local canals, flowering rush (inset) blooms from July to August in wet habitats.*

FACT FILE

- ✳ 3 miles (4.8 km) north-east of Macclesfield

- ⊡ Pathfinder 759 (SJ 87/97), grid reference SJ 931781

  miles 0 1 2 3 4 5 6 7 8 9 10 miles
  kms 0 1 2 3 4 5 6 7 8 9 10 11 12 13 14 15 kms

- ◔ Allow 2 hours

- ▬ Steep hill climb at beginning then gradual descent, followed by level canal walking. Mainly well defined paths, some road walking; walking boots advised

- P North-western edge of Bollington, close to the Middlewood Way and Macclesfield Canal; just off the B5090 road

- ⌂ Numerous inns passed on walk — Vale Inn, Queens Arms, and Red Lion Inn in Bollington. On the canal the Barge Inn

- WC In car park

- I Information centre at Adelphi Mill. Information and Ranger centre at car park

A bracing walk to a vantage point over the Cheshire Plain

The route is on field paths and along towpaths and after the initial steep ascent is mostly level walking. White Nancy **B** and the Saddle of Kerridge is an exceptional vantage point with extensive views over the Cheshire Plain. Being the end of the Pennines the hills make a dramatic rise from the plain. Along these hills you follow a section of the Gritstone Trail **C** before descending to the canal, passing mills, aqueducts and narrowboats.

The town of Bollington **A** is dominated by the 1,000-foot (305-metre) high ridge of Kerridge. There were numerous mills here that were driven by power from the many streams and later by coal carried on the canal. The last cotton mill ceased operating in 1960. Many of the mills and houses are built from stone quarried from Kerridge Hill.

The prominent and renowned landmark of White Nancy is a cylindrical white painted dome. It is believed to have been built by the Gaskell family to commemorate the Battle of Waterloo. Nancy was a member of the family.

The full route of the Gritstone Trail, which you follow for a short

THE WALK

BOLLINGTON – MACCLESFIELD CANAL

The walk begins in Bollington **A**, *from Adlington Road car park beside the Middlewood Way. Most of it is walked in a clockwise direction.*

➤ Walk out of the car park and turn right along Adlington Road to main road junction and turn left along Palmerston Street. Walk under the Bollington Aqueduct and turn right along Water Street to its junction with High Street beside the Queens Arms. Turn right along High Street ascending to the Red Lion Inn. Turn left and at the end of the row of houses (at the start of Cow Lane) is the path sign and stile for White Nancy and Saddle of Kerridge.

2 Turn right and ascend steeply, close to the field boundary on your right, to a stile. Go through this and take a flight of stone steps to the next stile, just ahead through the wall on the left and continue your ascent. Cross a track and continue ascending to the white-topped monument — White Nancy **B**. (This is steep and can be slippery in wet weather so footwear should have a good grip.)

3 Walk along the crest of the Saddle of Kerridge (part of the Gritstone Trail **C**) with the wall on your left to a stile. Continue, after 27 yards (25 metres) cross wall using obvious stile. After this keep the wall on your right along the crest to the next stile. Then keep wall on left and continue until three field walls converge at a stile. Don't cross the stile, but turn right at the 'Danger – Fenced Quarry Face' sign. Descend the path by the wall to a stile and continue descending with an old (Endon) quarry on your right, down to the old quarry track. Turn left to a minor road.

4 Cross over minor road and take footpath signposted to your right and walk down the track towards Endon Hall. Just before the first buildings turn sharp left and continue on the track to its end. Go through the waymarked wooden stile to the right and keep the wall on your left. At the end of the wall, 219 yards (200 metres) after the stile, turn right and cross field to a wooden stile in a fence. Cross the next field to another stile and the next field to the left-hand side of the castellated gatehouse of Endon Hall, where there is a stile into the lane.

5 Turn left along lane (Oak Lane) to the Macclesfield Canal ¼ mile (400 metres) away **D**. Cross the canal; descend the left-hand side of the crossover Bridge No. 29 and follow the towpath on the left-hand side of canal for the next 1½ miles (2.4 km) to Bridge No. 26.

En route you will pass a marina on your right; Adelphi Mill **E** with information centre. Then cross Bollington Aqueduct. Here, leave the canal and turn left along road (take care with children as no pavement) and descend back to car park that is crossed by Middlewood Way viaduct **F**.

◀ *A crossover bridge on the Macclesfield Canal, built to enable the horse pulling the boat to cross without unhitching.*

locks. It forms a part of the 97-mile (156-km) Cheshire Ring canal circuit. By the 1950s it was little used but with the restoration of the Peak Forest and Ashton canals the canal became used again and is today one of the most attractive skirting the base of the Pennine Hills. While walking along the canal Adelphi Mill **E** is passed. Built in 1856 it was originally a cotton mill but closed in the 1970s. The gatehouse is now an information centre.

The car park at the end of the walk is beside the Middlewood Way **F**. The way — 11 miles (18 km) long from Marple to Macclesfield — has been created from the former railway line, the M, B and M Railway (Macclesfield, Bollington and Macclesfield). The line opened in the 1860s and closed in 1970. In 1985 it was re-opened as a pedestrian, cycling and horse-riding route.

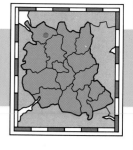

THE CLOUD AND THE BRIDESTONES

2

CHESHIRE

To a foothill of the Pennines with outstanding views

On the border between Cheshire and Staffordshire stands the Cloud (sometimes called Bosley Cloud), one of the foothills of the Pennines. Standing 1,125 feet (343 metres) above sea level, it provides an excellent vantage point over both counties plus the hills of Shropshire, Wales and the Pennines.

Woods, fields, bare hills, quarries, reservoirs, villages and towns are all laid out at your feet. So reserve this walk for a fine day, preferably after

MIKE WILLIAMS. INSET:L. CAMPBELL/NHPA

FACT FILE

- ☀ Timbersbrook, South Cheshire, 2 miles (3.2 km) east of Congleton

- os Pathfinder 776 (SJ 86/96), grid reference SJ 894627

  miles 0 1 2 3 4 5 6 7 8 9 10 miles
  kms 0 1 2 3 4 5 6 7 8 9 10 11 12 13 14 15 kms

- ◓ Allow 3 hours

- ◣ Steep sections, rough surface in places. Walking shoes or boots are recommended

- P Timbersbrook Picnic Area

- 🍽 Refreshments in Congleton, Biddulph or one of the many pubs on the main A roads in the area

- T For up-to-date bus information, Tel. (01270) 505350

rain has cleared any haze from the atmosphere, for the best views.

The walk begins at Timbersbrook Picnic Area **Ⓐ**. You are at the foot of the Cloud at 525 feet (160 metres). Timbersbrook takes its name from Timbers Brook, one of the many streams and rivers to provide water power for mills in the area. Textiles have been associated with this corner of Cheshire for over a hundred years and water power was important for the mills. Water was also needed in large quantities during

▲ *On the ascent to the Cloud, circling the woods at Cloud Plantation, there are dramatic views west over the Cheshire plain. The inedible rufous milk cap (inset) grows under conifers.*

the dyeing process. The picnic area is on the site of an old dyeworks.

As you walk up the lane towards Gosberryhole Lane, you will see water running down the side of the road — numerous springs arise at this level, where the porous gritstone of the Cloud meets the

THE WALK

TIMBERSBROOK

The walk starts at Timbersbrook picnic area Ⓐ and car park, off Weathercock Lane.

1 Walk through the car park to the five-bar gate and pedestrian entrance to the picnic field. Walk across the flat grassy picnic area. It is not obvious where the footpath goes at first because trees obscure the exit, but walk past the picnic tables and head for some steps to the right of the furthest picnic table. Walk up these steps to the road (be careful of traffic).

2 Turn left and walk uphill.

3 After about ¼ mile (400 metres) you will see Gosberryhole Lane (a rough track) leading off to the right, opposite Acorn Lane. Turn onto Gosberryhole Lane and follow it uphill.

4 Soon after passing Folly Cottage on your right, you will see that the track divides, with the left choice leading uphill past a National Trust sign. Take this steeper track, which ascends to join another track from your right. Turn left and continue uphill.

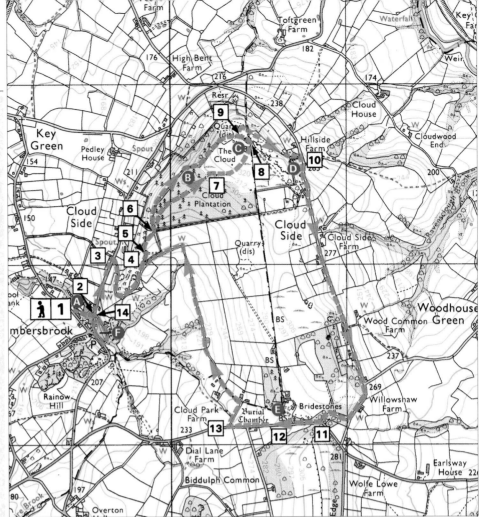

5 The track curves round to the right; here you can make a slight detour onto one of the narrow footpaths through the heather. This leads to the edge of crags and gives you a good view over Timbersbrook and the countryside beyond. Return to track and follow it to the woods, where you pass through a gap in the boundary wall/fence.

6 Here paths radiate outwards in all directions; you can choose either the left-hand path to walk along the edge of the wood Ⓑ, giving fine views of the Cheshire plain, or the broader track straight ahead and running parallel to the path, which takes you through the wood.

7 Eventually you emerge from the wood into an open area of heather and follow the obvious path upwards. All the paths lead to the triangulation pillar at the highest point of the Cloud Ⓒ.

8 From the pillar, take the path leading westwards along the top of the crag (that is, if standing facing the drop, with the heather plateau behind you, take the path on your left). When the path begins to

---

▲ *Timbersbrook lies at the foot of the Cloud. The picnic area here was once the site of a dye-works for textiles.*

ALL PHOTOS MIKE WILLIAMS

layer of glacial clay that covers much of the Cheshire Plain.

Once you leave Gosberryhole Lane and begin to climb more steeply up the rough track past the National Trust sign, you will notice how the vegetation changes. The height — 800 feet (244 metres) — affects the success of different plants. Here, bilberry bushes form neat hedges alongside the path, heather and bracken clothe the ground and small silver birch and mountain ash provide perches for the songbirds.

As you walk through the wood Ⓑ, look out for goldcrests, jays, chiffchaffs and spotted flycatchers in the summer. Once you emerge onto the heather moor, you may see meadow pipits and cuckoos.

FINE VIEWS

Once on top of the Cloud Ⓒ, the views are outstanding. Looking back over the woods, you can see an undulating woody ridge leading away from you, the end marked by a radio mast. With binoculars you can see the sham castle of Mow Cop, built in 1754, to the left of the mast.

To the left of the ridge, you can see the small town of Biddulph, which is north of the Potteries conurbation. To the right of the

lead away from the edge back to the wood, keep near to the edge and note where the outcrop of rocks ends and flat heather-clad ground begins.

9 You can scramble down beside these rocks to reach the grassy platform at their base, or walk another 26 yards (24 metres) to find the footpath leading down to the foot of the rocks. Once under rocks, do not take the level path beneath them, but with care scramble down a steep path slightly to the left, to join an obvious path running around the hillside below you. When you

reach this path, turn right. Follow it down past a stone cottage to the lane, crossing two stiles on way.

10 Turn right onto the lane **D** (traffic regularly uses it). Walk along the lane for about 1 mile (1.6 km), passing the junction with the lane to Woodhouse Green. When you see a stone farmhouse on the left-hand side of lane, look out for a right turn and take it. This leads you to a T-junction with a much busier road, where you turn right.

11 Walking along the verge, you will pass a large house with beautiful grounds (Bridestones).

Then you will see a farm drive on your right that hugs the garden's boundary wall. Walk along here. On your left is a field and, where the field hedge stops and a row of yew trees begins, look for a gate that leads through the trees to the burial chamber known as The Bridestones **E**.

12 Retrace your steps along the drive to the road and turn right.

13 Take next right turn along a lane (the other end of Gosberryhole Lane, although not marked). Follow this lane that starts off being tarmac, but soon reverts to stony track. After 1 mile (1.6 km), you

will recognize the section of track that you were on earlier. At the road, opposite Acorn Lane, turn left and walk downhill.

14 At the stile on the right which leads back into the picnic area, cross the road to a gate marked 'Poolside walk'. Go through gate; take the right-hand path crossing a wooden footbridge and walk alongside the reservoir **F**. Emerge onto a road, turn right onto it, then right at the T-junction and cross the road when you see a gap in the fence. This gap in the fence leads into the picnic field again via a shallow flight of steps.

▶ *Heather and bracken grow among the rocks on this steep part of the walk, which approaches the plantation area belonging to the National Trust.*

Nature Walk

MIKE WOODS

In flight, THE JAY is easily recognized by its white rump above its black tail. Wingbeats are weak.

ridge, the land sweeps down to the Cheshire Plain and in the distance you can see the Shropshire hills.

As you turn your gaze to the right, you can see the small town of Congleton in the foreground, perhaps with sunlight glinting on Astbury Mere, an old sand quarry now filled with water. Working sand quarries show up brightly across the plain — silica sand deposits are highly valued by industry.

Further to the right you can see

the radio telescope at Jodrell Bank. Power station cooling towers and the white buildings of Manchester Airport are visible on clear days too.

Looking over the edge of the Cloud to the left of the triangulation pillar, you can see the railway viaduct below you which crosses the Dane Valley. This viaduct carries the main line from Stoke-on-Trent to Macclesfield and then Manchester.

Beyond the viaduct, you can see a wooded hill standing above the plain — this is Alderley Edge. King

▼*The patchwork appearance of these drystone walls is a result of repair. The old stones are black from lichen.*

▲ *This stony track leads from the burial chamber; in summertime the woods and verges are full of wild flowers.*

Arthur's knights are reputed to sleep beneath this hill.

An obvious landmark is the telecommunications tower in front of you on Bosley Minn, with Bosley reservoir below. This is a British Waterways Board reservoir, used to keep the canal systems topped up. To the right of the tower is a range of hills in the Peak National Park. At 1,834 feet (559 metres), Shining Tor in the distance is the highest point in Cheshire. The flat-topped mound is Shutlingsloe and the craggy ridge to the right is the Roaches, a popular climbing area. To the right of the Roaches the land dips, then rises to form a sharply pointed hill called Hen Cloud. Further to the right is

▼ *This tranquil pool near the end of the walk was made by damming a brook to provide ample water for a dye-works.*

Communal Burial Chamber

The Bridestones (once called the Catstones) is a burial chamber with a semi-circular forecourt and stone façade, known as a court cairn. Similar structures, which have been dated, suggest that this one was built during the new stone age (Neolithic), probably around 2,500 BC. During the Neolithic period (3,500 – 1,800 BC), people began the slow transition from hunting and gathering to settled farming, and burial places are associated with a more settled way of life.

Archaeologists think that this chamber was a communal one, holding the cremated remains of between 10 and 50 individuals, who could have been successive generations of the same family.

Unfortunately the stone has been robbed over the centuries for roadmaking and other uses. But you can still make out the main chamber of gritstone slabs, divided in two by another slab. This is broken, but was originally a large slab with a 19½ inch

(50 cm) diameter porthole in it. The chamber would have been 6 feet (1.8 metres) high inside and, when first described in 1766, there was a semi-circular facade of six to eight upright stones, about 6 feet (1.8 metres) apart, with two stones within on the paved forecourt. Two more uprights were mentioned at the eastern angle of the chamber. The whole structure would then have been closed off with a massive cairn, or stone.

The Bridestones, the remains of a burial chamber believed to date from Neolithic times, is now moss-covered and overgrown with bracken and wild shrubs.

Leek and you can just make out the town's buildings beyond Rudyard Reservoir. Rudyard Kipling's parents named him after this place.

BIRD LIFE OF THE MOOR

After you have absorbed the view, turn your attention to the heather moor behind you and see if you can spot any finches, redpolls, linnets or

perhaps a bird of prey. The drystone wall that marches away from you into the distance marks the county boundary: Cheshire to your right and Staffordshire to your left.

When you reach the lane **D**, you still have extremely good views across the wide Dane valley. Also, you can admire the hamlet of Cloud Side, with its chapel above you and on the right.

WOOD PLANTATION

Having explored The Bridestones (a stone burial chamber) **E** and continued to Gosberryhole Lane, you have views of the Cloud's plantation through the trees that line this lane. You may see redwings and fieldfares on the fields in winter and, in early summer, bluebells by the lane.

On your return to Timbersbrook, you make a final detour around a pool **F**. There is a seat here for you to rest and look across the water.

TEGG'S NOSE SUMMIT

MIKE WILLIAMS. INSET: DUNCAN I. MCEWAN/AQUILA

Around reservoirs and a country park with splendid views

This walk takes you through a quarry that was closed in 1955 and has since been reclaimed by nature. It is now a country park.

You start at the Visitor Centre car park, where you can gaze over drystone-walled fields and the town of Macclesfield. The area is high,

▲*A panoramic view from the summit of Tegg's Nose, with Teggsnose and Bottoms reservoirs below. Purple heather (inset) grows on heath and moorland and flowers in late summer.*

1,148 feet (350 metres) above sea level, and exposed — the quarry you have parked on and the house above it are called Windy Way. The plants have to be tough and low-growing; bilberry and heather with shrubby willow and some hawthorn predominate alongside the grasses.

MILLSTONE GRIT

The hills around are of millstone grit, a type of sandstone that was valued for millstones (hence its name) and had many other uses. The quarrying exhibition ❹ illustrates the various uses of the stone quarried in this area. A stone building and stone wall enclose an area of exhibits of quarrymen's products. The building houses information on the geology of the cliff facing you, plus a display of quarrymen's tools.

◄*A vertical ascent up the sheer rock face left after the quarrying activity.*

MIKE WILLIAMS

FACT FILE

* Tegg's Nose Country Park, 2 miles (3.2 km) east of Macclesfield

* Outdoor Leisure Map 24, grid reference SJ 950732

miles 0 1 2 3 4 5 6 7 8 9 10 miles
kms 0 1 2 3 4 5 6 7 8 9 10 11 12 13 14 15 kms

* Allow at least 2 hours

* Paths steep in places, muddy after rain; walking shoes are recommended

* **P** Free car park at Tegg's Nose Country Park Visitor Centre

* **T** BR station at Macclesfield. Bus information, Tel. Cheshire Bus Line (01270) 505350. Special summer service

* In Macclesfield and at Langley, Sutton, Walker Barn and Ridgegate Reservoir

* Refreshments at Visitor Centre at weekends. Café at Macclesfield

* **WC** Visitor Centre

THE WALK

TEGG'S NOSE COUNTRY PARK

The walk begins at the car park by Tegg's Nose Country Park Visitor Centre.

1 Walk back to the road from the car park, past the Visitor Centre. At the road, turn left onto the footpath that runs alongside the road and is signposted to Croker Hill and Tegg's Nose summit. At the kissing gate, enter a field with a clearly defined path along its edge. Walk along the footpath and leave the field by another kissing gate.

2 Turn left here and walk uphill on a stony track. Keep on the stony track, walking through the heather-covered spoil heaps. Eventually you will arrive at a cliff with an exhibition **A** of quarry machinery and stone products at its foot.

3 Having examined the exhibition, continue along the track, which takes you by the side of a deep quarry **B** with vertical faces.

4 The track continues to hug this hole, curving around to the right. But at this point, look for a footpath leading straight on that is part of the Gritstone Trail. (The Gritstone Trail runs from Lyme Park to Rushton Spencer, passing through the Country Park. The symbol of the trail is a footprint with the letter G on it.) This path takes you

to an open area and if you make a short detour to the left, to a small square boulder and a seat 20 yards (18 metres) further on, you will be able to see Ridgegate Reservoir **C** and The Leather Smithy pub.

5 Back on the main footpath you come to a flat area after a few paces and find yourself at the junction of many paths leading off in all directions. If you turn left along a level, broad path, you will arrive at a viewpoint **D**, information board and seat. From here you can see Teggsnose **E** and Bottoms **F** Reservoirs and the village of Langley.

6 Return to the footpath junction and take the broad, level path that sweeps around to your right to a post and wire fence. One of the fenceposts has the Gritstone Trail waymarker fixed to it.

7 Stay on this level path by the fence until you see a stile on the left, marked with the Gritstone Trail symbol. The path descends some steps, then continues down a grassy slope with gorse and bramble patches. (Care here for those who wear shorts!) This obvious path descends to Teggsnose Wood, where steps and a handrail are provided. Do not be tempted to take any paths on the left across the slope.

8 At the bottom of the steps you pass an information board and

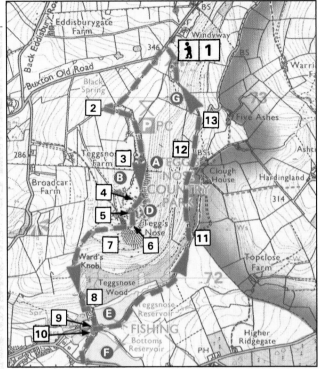

enter a small car-parking area at the end of Teggsnose Reservoir's dam. Walk along the dam and turn left at the tarmacked lane, where the signpost indicates a bridlepath.

9 Look for a pedestrian gate in the wall on your right, waymarked Gritstone Trail. Go through the gate and walk along the dam of Bottoms Reservoir, where you may see some interesting birds and where you have a good view across Langley. Retrace your steps to the gate and then turn right onto the tarmacked lane.

10 Walk along the lane with its views into Teggsnose Reservoir. If you look up to your left, you will see spoil from the quarry, below the viewpoint.

11 When you reach a footpath (waymarked with

a stone sign to Forest Chapel car park) leading straight on, where the lane curves to the right take the footpath down to Walker Barn stream. Cross by the stepping stones and take the footpath on the left leading uphill to a stile on the left. Cross the stile and turn right to walk along the fence. Cross another stile and walk along a footpath which joins the farm track, where there is another stile to negotiate, next to a gate. Clough House Farm is on your right.

12 When you reach the tarmacked lane, turn left uphill. Look up and left and you will see the top of the hoist from the quarry exhibition in Stage 2.

13 Where the lane curves to the right, continue straight ahead along the stone-surfaced bridlepath (Saddlers Way **G**), which leads back to the car park.

Outside, there is machinery typical of a quarry — a stone saw and a stone crusher. Further on you will see the deep hole **B** left here by quarrying operations and the sheer face used by rock-climbers.

The information board at the viewpoint **D** tells you about the geology of the area and the reservoirs. The larger Ridgegate Reservoir **C** is for drinking water and the two small ones (Teggsnose **E** and Bottoms **F**) were built to keep the level of Bollin River topped up once

Ridgegate reduced its levels.

Saddlers Way **G** is an old packhorse route, one of many that used to criss-cross the area. It was re-surfaced between 1984 and 1987 and there is a plaque part-way along it providing information.

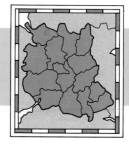

ROBERT EAMES. INSET: NATURE PHOTOGRAPHERS

Nether Alderley, 4 miles (6.4 km) north-west of Macclesfield, on the A34

os Pathfinder 759 (SJ 87/97), grid reference SJ 841761

miles 0 1 2 3 4 5 6 7 8 9 10 miles
kms 0 1 2 3 4 5 6 7 8 9 10 11 12 13 14 15 kms

Allow 3 hours

Field and woodland paths and lanes, with some gentle climbs

P Roadside by St Mary's Church

T Buses between Manchester and Macclesfield pass Nether Alderley Mill, Tel. (01625) 534850. BR station ½ mile (800 m) north of Stage 4, on the A34

Wizard Restaurant and Tea Rooms. A variety of pubs and cafés etc in Alderley Edge

I National Trust Information Centre, Tel. (01625) 584412

Past ponds rich in wildlife to a hillside steeped in folklore

▲Nether Alderley Mill was grinding corn in the 15th century. Sweet vernal grass (inset), which gives hay its characteristic scent, grows in the meadows around St Mary's Church.

The Edge at Alderley Edge is one of the first geological rumblings that mark the transition from the low-lying Cheshire Plain to the heights of the Peak District and the Pennine backbone of England. A great wedge of wooded sandstone, it is an area steeped in folklore, and with a long history of human settlement.

Sweeping views stretch across to the Dark Peak of Derbyshire, and over Manchester to the towering knuckles of gritstone that form the West Pennine Moors in Lancashire. Old copper and lead workings pockmark the Edge, while, on the plain below, the walk passes an ancient church and a medieval corn mill.

The 700-year-old St Mary's Church at Nether Alderley Ⓐ, where the walk begins, retains many 13th-century features, including a font lost for nearly 300 years after it was buried to protect it from Puritan troops in the Civil War. Inside the church are monuments to the Stanley family, Lords of the Manor, and an unusual family pew, rather like a theatre box. The old village school, which dates from 1628, is next to the lychgate, and the churchyard is surrounded by flower-rich hay meadows.

PONDS AND MERES

Jodrell Bank Radio Telescope is visible across the plain to the south-west as you head north to a pond Ⓑ, which is alive with tadpoles in spring and dragonflies during the summer. Hundreds of similar ponds have been filled in during the past 200 years, while adjoining marshy land has been drained. Cheshire is dotted with meres, ponds and marshes, most of them a legacy of the last Ice Age, 10,000 years ago.

A gentle climb through Manchester's 'Broker Belt' takes you above the town of Alderley Edge. At the foot of a sandstone bluff is Wizard's Well Ⓒ. According to local legend,

▲Gaps in the trees on Alderley Edge provide views across the plain.

the Wizard is guardian of an army of knights on white horses, sleeping in a vast underground cavern while they await the call to come to the rescue of a beleaguered England. The children's author Alan Garner based his tales The Weirdstone of Brisangamen and The Moon of Gomrath on this area and its folklore. Near the well is the Beacon Ⓓ, site of one of the chain of beacons lit to warn of the coming of the Spanish

ROBERT EAMES

THE WALK

NETHER ALDERLEY – ALDERLEY EDGE

The start of the walk is at St Mary's Church A, Nether Alderley.

▶ Cross the stiles just beyond the church tower, then cross the field to a large fingerpost. Follow the path for Chorley and Walton Farm. Cross the road and go along a wide path opposite. Cross the footbridge and head slightly left towards a red-brick farmhouse in the middle distance. Cross a stile near the field corner, then take the line of stiles to a minor road.

▶ Turn right then immediately left down a track towards Walton Farm. Just before it, climb the stile beside an old bath on your right. Follow the line of hedge over two more stiles, then turn left to the corner of the field. Turn right, and shortly right again alongside an isolated hedgerow in the middle of the field. At the far end, go left by a home-made footpath sign just before the railway, passing some gnarled trees to reach the corner by the two massive elms.

▶ Climb the stile to the left of a pond B, and join the course of a brook on your right. Recross the brook to climb the stile beside a metal gate on your right, and cross the field to a railway bridge. Follow the path beyond to the edge of a modern housing estate. At a footpath sign, turn right to reach a main road.

▶ Go right, then left up Beechfield Road. At a sharp bend right, go straight on up the old drive of the mansion, Serotina. Immediately before two brick gateposts, turn right and follow a fenced pathway to its end, crossing an estate road on the way. Turn left, then follow the drive towards White Barn Farm. Where this surfaced drive curves right, go straight ahead along a rough track and onto an area of heathland.

▶ About 50 yards (45m) after the gate, turn left and follow the path through overgrown old copper workings. Pass by a small pond to your left to a stile. Do not cross, but turn right and walk up alongside and past the woods to a road (the B5087). Go straight over and along a short path to reach the Edge at Alderley. Bear left to find Wizard's Well C, then backtrack and walk along the Edge to the beacon D and mines.

▶ Bear right to go roughly south through the woods, always following the major path, for about ½ mile (800m) to a large car park by the Wizard Restaurant and the National Trust hut. Turn left along the B5087, then right by some chevrons, along a minor road.

▶ At a fork, bear right towards the Holiday Park. Ignore the park entrance and keep left, remaining with the track, then cobbled road, to reach the A34 after about 1 mile (1.6km). Turn left to Nether Alderley Mill E. Just beyond it, turn right down a narrow road to return to the start.

Armada in 1588. The Beacon Tower fell in a gale in the 1930s.

The Edge, richly clothed in beech, oak and Scots pine trees, was given by the Pilkington family to the National Trust in the 1940s. On certain days of the year, the Trust allows a local caving club to guide members of the public through some of the old copper and lead mines that honeycomb the sandstone and cut shallow gorges in its surface. A small information centre outlines the area's mining history.

The National Trust is also the guardian of Nether Alderley Mill E,

ROBERT EAMES

towards the end of the walk, which was recently restored after several decades of dereliction. The enormous, steeply pitched slab tiles hide machinery little changed from that which first ground corn in the time of the Wars of the Roses. The mill is not, as it seems at first glance, built into the hillside; uniquely, the back wall of the mill also acts as the dam to a millpond situated immediately behind the building.

◀*Wizard's Well, on Alderley Edge, has become part of local folklore that links it with an army of sleeping knights.*

◀*The Valeroyal Cut of the Weaver Navigation, once a busy industrial route, is now a quiet water, frequented by anglers who cast their lines for fish such as the leather carp (inset).*

DEREK PRATT. INSET. LUTRA/NHPA

The adjoining ponds, parts of the old river, are rich in birdlife. The keeper at Valeroyal Locks **E**, a keen ornithologist, spreads news of the latest sightings and rarities via the lock-side noticeboard. The locks, among the largest in Britain, are now rarely used. The Anderton Boat Lift, near Northwich, is under long-term repair, and this peaceful backwater is all but isolated.

LODGE AND ABBEY

There are views across meadows to the imposing mansion of Vale Royal **F**, a remodelled remnant of a vast Cistercian abbey, by far the largest in England. Founded in 1277 by Edward I, it was never completely finished. After the Dissolution (1534) it was home to various noble families, but later fell into ruin. It has only recently been refurbished and reopened as a training centre.

An even more famous family sometimes used Cassia Lodge **G**, near the end of the walk, as a base. During World War II, George VI and his family came here to escape, for a time, the trials of London in the Blitz. A contemporary houseguest was General Eisenhower, who often stayed here while visiting American servicemen based nearby.

▼*The Valeroyal Locks were built large for the coasters that plied the canal.*

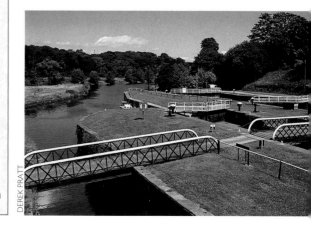

DEREK PRATT

A track bed, canalside and footpath walk in central Cheshire

The geographical heart of Cheshire is also the centre of the county's (as well as the country's) salt mining industry. This walk offers a glimpse of this old industry, and makes the most of Cheshire's rich agricultural and ecclesiastical heritage.

The walk begins in the old station yard **A** at Whitegate, now the car park for the Whitegate Way, a footpath and nature trail along the old railway. One of Dr Beeching's victims in the 1960s, the line was built to transport salt from the mines to the main line a few miles away.

An old moated area **B**, just off the line, is all that remains of Marton Grange. Bricks and stones from its walls were used in local farmhouses, such as adjoining Marton Hall Farm.

Small ponds on either side of the line are resplendent with rushes and yellow flag irises in the summer. Nearby woodland shimmers with the whites of anemones and ramsons, and vivid bluebells in season.

At the end of the Whitegate Way, you emerge into a landscape of small, bare mounds, glistening in places as the sun catches crystals of salt. This is Winsford Salt Mine **C**, one of the largest in Cheshire. Brown rocksalt, mined from underground caverns, is sold as road salt or to the chemical industry. Table salt is made in a different way; it is pumped from underground as brine and then separated by evaporation.

You descend to the Valeroyal Cut **D** of the Weaver Navigation. This peaceful wooded stretch also owes its existence to salt. The River Weaver was straightened, widened and deepened so that large coastal steamers could carry bulk rocksalt to the Mersey, and out to sea.

FACT FILE

* Whitegate, 3 miles (4.8km) south-west of Northwich

* Pathfinders 775 (SJ 66/76) and 758 (SJ 67/77), grid reference SJ 614680

  miles 0 1 2 3 4 5 6 7 8 9 10 miles
  kms 0 1 2 3 4 5 6 7 8 9 10 11 12 13 14 15 kms

* Allow 3 to 4 hours

* Level walking on old railway, field tracks, lanes and waterside. Some sections can be overgrown

* **P** Car park at the start

* The Plough Inn, Foxtwist Green

THE WALK

WHITEGATE

The walk begins from the old station car park **A***, 1¼ miles (2km) south-west of Whitegate village.*

1 From the far end of the car park, follow the well maintained Whitegate Way, passing by Marton Moat **B** off to your right. Follow the old railway line to its far end and turn left along the road.

2 About ¼ mile (400m) past Winsford Salt Mine **C**, turn right down some steps and across the bridges over the Weaver. Turn left and follow Valeroyal Cut **D** downstream to Valeroyal Locks **E**. Cross the bridges over the lock chambers and follow the rough road away from the Cut. Cross the old River Weaver and immediately go left through the anglers' car park and walk along the old driveway beyond.

3 As a neck of woodland appears on your right, go over the waymarked stile beside old wooden gates on your left. After a few paces, veer right through a hay meadow. Follow the river upstream, into broadleaf woodland, part of the Vale Royal estate **F**. Leave the woods via a stile at the far end and turn right along the line of oaks across the vast field. Climb the waymarked stile beneath the large oak at the far corner of the woods and keep the hedge to your right.

4 After about 300 yards (270m), climb the stile on your right and walk almost to the far end of the woods ahead. Go left over the stile and walk up just inside these woods. Leave the trees via the stile on your right. Walk round the old marl hole, then follow the field road, initially alongside woods, to a minor road. Turn right.

5 Go through the gate immediately left of the 'Grange Lane' nameboard and down the edge of the bungalow's garden. Though not marked, this is a public footpath. Cross the footbridge and head for the top left of the field. Pass through the gap left by an old field gate and turn right. Follow the field edges towards the black and white house in the middle distance. Several stiles bring you to a garden. Skirt this on your right to reach a minor road. Turn right.

6 After about 200 yards (180m), take the footpath left for Beauty Bank. Cross the footbridge in the valley and follow the line of stiles up the fields beyond to emerge from a gap between houses onto a road. Turn right. Pass The Plough Inn and go straight over the road at the end. At the end of this lane bear right at Cassia Green, passing Cassia Lodge **G**, then go left at the crossroads along Clay Lane to return to the starting point at Whitegate Station.

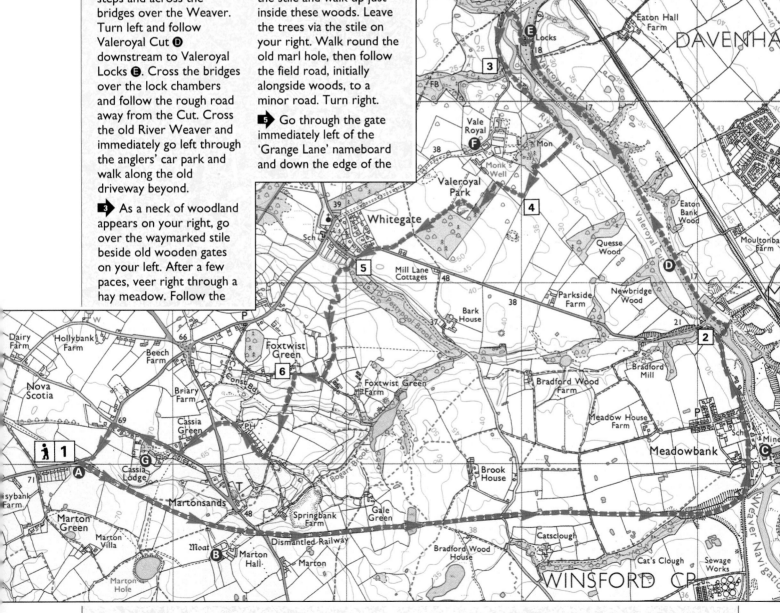

CRESWELL CRAGS

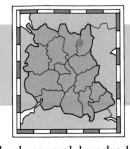

origins date back several hundred years. In 1538, Welbeck Abbey was the seat of the White Canons of a religious order founded in France. Later, the land came into the Shrewsbury and Cavendish family who owned the nearby Bolsover Castle and Hardwick Hall. The Abbey **Ⓐ** is now Welbeck College and the impressive house and estate is mostly the work of the Dukes of Portland. The riding school, as with the whole building, is built on a grand scale. In the 1700s, the Duke of Portland engaged the painter George Stubbs to paint views of the Welbeck Estate. One painting known as *Two Gentlemen Going Shooting* shows the mill and the crags.

CRAG'S POND

At the southern end of Crag's Pond **Ⓑ** is Crag's Cottage, once the Star Inn and the last building of a small settlement by a watermill. The mill and thatched buildings were later

▲ *The impressive limestone gorge of Creswell Crags contains a series of caves and rock shelters. (inset) The aggressive coot builds its substantial nest of reeds above the level of the water.*

Through woodland to a magnificent limestone gorge

The Creswell Crags are dramatic limestone cliffs that lie on either side of a narrow gorge, which serves as the boundary between Derbyshire and Nottinghamshire. This is one of the main places in Britain for palaeontology — the study of fossils.

THE LIMESTONE GORGE

The walk takes you through pleasant woodland before curving round to enter the gorge. Here, on either side of a pond, there are caves which were known to early man. Metal grids across their openings prevent access. The gorge is a Site of Special Scientific Interest (SSSI) for its geology and natural history. A variety of wild flowers and birds will be seen on the walk and the caves are a home for bats.

The crags and pond were once part of the Welbeck Estate, whose

FACT FILE

⊛ Creswell Crags is 1 mile (1.6 km) east of the village of Creswell on the B6042 road, between A616 and A60

▭ Pathfinder 762 (SK 47/57), grid reference SK 538743

| miles 0 | 1 | 2 | 3 | 4 | 5 | 6 | 7 | 8 | 9 | 10 miles |
| kms 0 | 1 2 3 4 | 5 | 6 7 | 8 | 9 10 11 | 12 13 14 | 15 kms |

◔ Allow 1–1½ hours

▭ Well defined level tracks and paths throughout. Wet in winter, so walking shoes or boots recommended.

Ⓟ Creswell Crags Visitors' Centre, just off the B6042 road. The car park closes at 5pm

Ⓣ Buses to Mansfield and Worksop stop at Creswell village

Toilets, refreshments and information at the car park.
WC Shops, restaurants and inns in Creswell village

Welbeck Abbey on Crag's Pond was originally built as a religious foundation in the 16th century. It is now Welbeck College.

THE WALK

CRESWELL CRAGS

The walk begins at the Creswell Crags Visitors' Centre car park and is walked in an anti-clockwise direction.

➡ Walk along the track away from the centre **A** and road to a bar gate in approximately 100 yards (90 metres).

➡ Turn left, as bridlepath signed, and follow a well-defined farm track (towards Hennymoor Farm). Just before the first field boundary (hedge) turn left and follow the grass track keeping the hedge on your right to reach a small gate and bridlepath sign at the minor road.

➡ Turn left and in 10 yards (9 metres) turn right on to another bridlepath with a metal bar gate. Keep on this well-defined track for a little

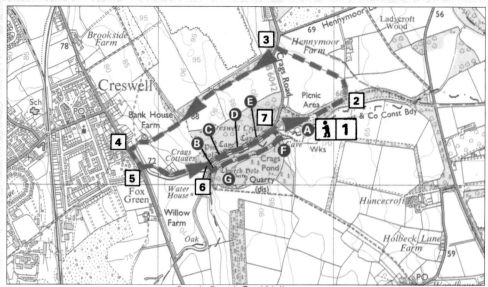

over ½ mile (0.6 km).

➡ Turn left beside the A616 road on the outskirts of Creswell village.

➡ Turn left along Crags Road (B6042).

➡ At the traffic lights turn right on to the path around

Crag's Pond **B**. Walk clockwise around the pond, duplicating the left-hand side path at the end to reach the opposite side of the pond. This walk round the pond takes in several caves: Pinhole Cave **C**, Robin Hood's Cave **D**, Mother

Grundy's Parlour **E**, Boat House Cave **F** and Church Hole Cave **G**.

➡ Follow path down the steps with the stream on your right which leads back to the Visitors' Centre and car park.

---

demolished in the 1860s as part of an extensive landscaping programme of the estate. The mill pond was drained and the lake, Crag's Pond, was made by damming the stream, to create a duck shooting lake for the Duke of Portland.

THE CAVES

It is not possible to go into the numerous caves that lie on either side of the pond, but a record of explorations and discoveries is displayed in an exhibition at the Visitors' Centre. Pin Hole Cave **C** was named after a 19th-century custom of each visitor placing a pin in the rock pool near the entrance. Excavations earlier this century have uncovered more than 15,000 pieces of bone. Evidence shows that man has occupied the cave intermittently over the last 45,000 years, and that hyenas used it as a den. Robin Hood's Cave **D** is the largest cave with four main chambers. Mother Grundy's Parlour **E** was named after a witch who lived there in the last century.

Boat House Cave **F**, as its name

indicates, was where the boat for the lake was kept. When the lake level was lowered in the 1930s, the cave was extensively excavated. The last cave on the walk, Church Hole Cave **G**, extends 170 feet (51 metres) into the hillside and has the finest artefacts from the area. Hyenas used it as their lair and bones from bison, bear, wolf, woolly rhinoceros, horse and cave lion have been found. The cave has been occupied by Neanderthal man, and pottery fragments show that it was also occupied in both Roman and medieval times.

◀ *In the 19th century the Welbeck estate was landscaped and Crag's Pond was drained to create a lake. (above) Boat House Cave, one of the numerous caves by the pond, which once served as a boat house.*

DERBYSHIRE

A pleasant and varied walk through 'the cradle of the Industrial Revolution'

At Cromford in 1771, Richard Arkwright established his own mill with its water-powered machinery and large workforce, earning him the title 'Father of the Factory System'. Cromford Canal was built to serve the mill. The area is rich in industrial archaeology, and the walk passes through attractive, hilly and wooded countryside which gives good views along the Derwent valley and across to the Peak District uplands. There are many interesting sites to visit and the canal is a rich area for wildlife and colourful wild flowers.

Cromford's uniquely historical Arkwright's mill **A** is well worth a visit either at the start or finish of the walk. Part of the mill is normally

FACT FILE

* Cromford, 18 miles (29km) north of Derby on the A6 and about 3 miles (4.8km) south of Matlock

* Outdoor Leisure Map 24: The Peak District White Peak Area, grid reference SK 299570

miles 0 1 2 3 4 5 6 7 8 9 10 miles
kms 0 1 2 3 4 5 6 7 8 9 10 11 12 13 14 15 kms

* Allow 2½ hours

* The towpath along the canal provides pleasant and easy walking at all times, and would be suitable for buggies or push chairs. The return route is hilly in places and some of the paths, although good and clear, could become muddy in wet weather, especially in the woods. There are several stiles and kissing gates

* **P** At Cromford Wharf

* Pubs and cafés in Cromford

▲ *Originally built to serve local industry, Cromford Canal is a haven for wildlife, like the moorhen (inset).*
▼ *Arkwright established his first cotton mill in the late 18th century.*

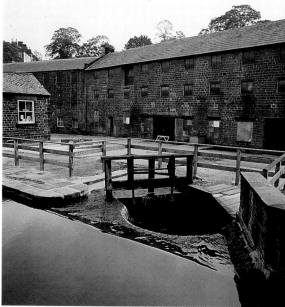

THE WALK

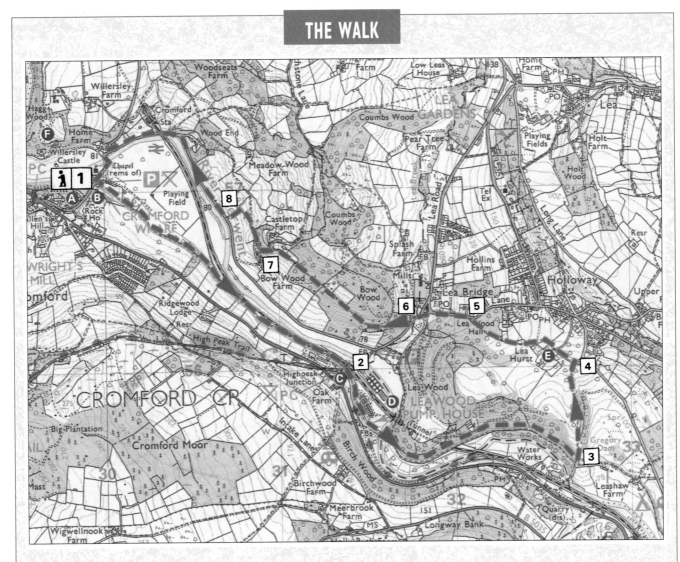

CROMFORD WHARF – LEA BRIDGE

The walk starts from the car park at Cromford Wharf just off the A6, 3 miles (4.8km) south of Matlock Bath.

1 From Cromford Wharf **B** start out along the towpath with the canal on your right. Continue for just over 1 mile (1.6 km) to High Peak Junction **C**.

2 After the junction, continue along the left bank of the canal past Leawood Pump House **D** and across the aqueduct over the River Derwent. At the end of the aqueduct, cross over by the swingbridge on to the right-hand bank of the canal. Follow the towpath for about ¾ mile (1km), to the canal tunnel.

3 At the tunnel entrance leave the towpath by taking the ascending path on the right to the top of the small hill. Turn left through the kissing gate and ascend the footpath ahead through the field, keeping to the left of the cottage. From the cottage follow the track by the high, stone wall to reach another kissing gate. Go through the gate.

4 Do not carry on along the track up to Holloway village, but turn left into the field and follow the hedgerow on your left. Cross over the drive which leads to Lea Hurst House **E** and continue along the left-hand hedge in the next small field. Go through a gap stile in the corner, then follow the stone wall round to reach a stile by a small copse. Follow the path through the trees then, keeping to the right, go down the field, over the stile and continue down the right-hand side of the next field to the kissing gate.

5 Turn left and follow the road down into Lea Bridge. (Take care when crossing the road because of the dangerous corner.) Cross the bridge over Lea Brook, to find the footpath on the right-hand side by the gate, near the corner of the mills.

6 Proceed through a stone gap stile and take the footpath bearing left into Bow Wood. Follow this main path through the wood, ignoring all paths to the left and right. Continue on the track leading out of the wood to reach the lane near Castletop Farm. Proceed through the stone gap stile.

7 Turn left down the lane, which affords good views of Willersley Castle across the valley. Follow the lane down to the road.

8 Turn right and follow the road along the bank of the River Derwent, back to the car park at Cromford Wharf, passing the entrance to Willersley Castle **F** and crossing the road bridge above the river.

open to the public, and includes a Visitor and Exhibition Centre, shops and a café for refreshments.

Before the coming of the railways the transport of bulky raw materials and merchandise was a considerable problem for the early industrialists and Cromford Canal **B** was built largely on the initiative of Richard Arkwright to serve his new mill, although it was not opened until 1793, a year after his death. It was designed by William Jessop, cost £80,000 at the time, to construct and ran for nearly 15 miles (24km) to join the Erewash Canal at Langley Mill, and so on to Derby and the River Trent. It was heavily used until the coming of the railway to Matlock in the 1860s. It then fell into decline and was eventually closed at the turn of the century.

HAVEN FOR WILDLIFE

This section of the canal has now been restored by the Cromford Canal Society and Derbyshire County Council. The area is now a rich sanctuary for wildlife. Look out

for mallards, coots, moorhens and mammals such as water shrews and voles. And in the summer months, there is a mass of wild flowers, including water forget-me-nots, water mint and water speedwell.

At High Peak Junction **C** goods were transferred to and from the canal on to the High Peak Railway, which was opened in 1831 at a cost of £185,000. It was built by Josiah Jessop, the son of William Jessop, and ran across the southern uplands of the Peak District to the Peak Forest Canal at Whalley Bridge. It reached a height of 1,264 feet (380 metres) at Ladmanlow and

NatureWalk

ROPE SLOT BRIDGES have a slot in the span to let the tow rope through. This saved unhitching the horse from the barge where the towpath changed sides.

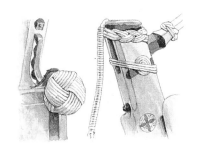

ROPEWORK is still seen on narrowboats. This has both a decorative and a practical function, cushioning the boat from knocks and providing a secure means of tying up alongside the canal.

◄ High Peak Junction, a busy transfer point for goods moving by water and rail.

▼ Willersley Castle, 'country seat' of the Arkwrights.

Lea Wood Pump House ensured that the canal never lacked water.

included nine inclines up which the wagons had to be hauled.

The 33 mile (53km) journey took two days. The long, steep Cromford incline from the canal up to Black Rock was worked by a stationary steam engine with an endless rope haulage system. The last section of the line was closed in 1967 and most of it has now been converted into the High Peak Walking Trail. There is a small information centre on the site and the restored workshops and warehouses are usually open to the public for viewing.

Leawood Pump House **D** was built in 1840 to pump water from the Derwent into the canal at times

Sir Richard Arkwright

Richard Arkwright was born in Preston, Lancashire, in 1732, the youngest of seven children born to a tailor. An inventive and enterprising man, he designed and built a machine for spinning cotton which, since it was powered by water, became known as the waterframe. His mill at Nottingham, built in 1769, used horsepower to drive the machinery, but this was incapable of further development on a large scale, so in his search for sufficient, continuous water power to drive his newly invented machinery, he moved to Cromford.

The first mill in Cromford was built in 1771, and it became the world's first successful, water-powered cotton spinning mill based on a factory system. By the 1780s, the mill was operating almost continuously, employing nearly 500 workers, usually working 12-hour shifts. The whole mill complex was completed in 1791. At the same time, Arkwright

▲ Arkwright started life as a wigmaker and barber. But he went on to develop machines (below) that revolutionised the textile industry.

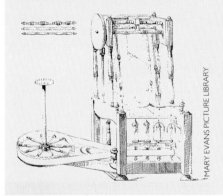

developed Cromford into one of the first industrial villages, with terraced rows of cottages for the mill workers. The new enterprise was immensely successful and Arkwright went on to build other mills elsewhere and to license machinery to other industrial entrepreneurs.

He amassed a great personal fortune, leaving £500,000 at his death — an enormous sum of money in those days. He was knighted in 1786 and was appointed High Sheriff of Derbyshire in 1787. He started to build a stately country house, Willersley Castle, but died in 1792, before it was completed.

the works and out of his industrial fortune, he built the imposing Hydro mansion in nearby Matlock Bath (which is now the Council Offices) and the even more grandiose Riber Castle which still dominates the town.

After Florence Nightingale's sterling work in the Crimean War, she

The now peaceful waters of the canal — a far cry from the busy waterway of earlier times.

made Lea Hurst her home, and it was here that she wrote numerous books on nursing and hospital organisation. The house is now a residential home for the elderly.

STATELY HOME

Sir Richard Arkwright lived initially at Rock House, which still stands near his first mill, but as his fortunes prospered, work began in 1788 on a more fitting baronial mansion, Willersley Castle **F**. Over £3,000 was spent at the outset, blasting out and excavating the rocky site. The building was almost completed, when it was badly damaged by fire in 1791.

Arkwright died in the following year and so never actually lived in the so-called castle. He is buried in a bricked-up vault in the nearby St Mary's Church, just by the bridge over the Derwent. This church was originally a private chapel and mausoleum for the Arkwright family. The castle is now a Methodist Church Conference Centre.

of shortage. Inside is the original Graham & Co. beam engine. It is presently being restored and is sometimes open to the public on Sundays in the summer months.

Lea Hurst House **E** is the family home of Florence Nightingale, 'The Lady with the Lamp'. Florence's family built and operated the cotton spinning mills at nearby Lea Bridge in the 1780s and Florence's father greatly enlarged the house in the early 19th century. The mills were later purchased and turned to hosiery manufacture by Thomas Smedley. His son John expanded

◄ The water shrew paralyses its prey with poisonous saliva.

THE LINACRE VALLEY

A short walk through quiet woodlands fringing three reservoirs

The old coal valleys in the Derbyshire Coalfield and east of the Peak District National Park tend to be overlooked by visitors from other areas of the country. This one, however, is well worth exploring, and is made particularly attractive by three bodies of water, the reservoirs that were formerly Chesterfield's only public water supply.

The route descends from the car park in Kitchenflat Wood, in medieval times the site of Linacre Hall. The hall was superseded by Linacre House, birthplace of Dr Thomas Linacre (1460-1524). An outstanding academic who numbered Sir Thomas More and Erasmus among his pupils, his formidable scholarship was commemorated in 1938 when new choir stalls in Old Brampton Church were dedicated to his memory.

Sadly, Linacre House has long since been demolished because of drainage problems caused by the creation of the lower reservoir in the Linacre Valley. (The old English word Linacre is derived from 'lin' meaning flax and 'acre' meaning land.)

ROGER REDFERN. INSET MAURICE K. WALKER/NATURE PHOTOGRAPHERS LTD

A typical view of a quiet woodland glade close to the middle reservoir.

ROGER REDFERN

The ambitious reservoir construction plan, conceived to supply all Chesterfield's water needs, was undertaken in the typically bold spirit that epitomised so many Victorian endeavours. Work began in 1855 with the construction of the smallest reservoir **G**. This was followed in 1863 by the largest reservoir **B**. The middle reservoir **A** was built in 1904. Although widely admired as a feat of engineering, the reservoirs and their wooded surroundings remained mysterious and little visited until the Severn Trent Water Board took over the valley in the 1970s. Since then the area has been opened to the public and car parks and picnic facilities provided.

BIRDS AND FLOWERS

Although artificial in origin, the reservoirs have become a natural home to all kinds of waterfowl; mallard, little grebe, moorhens and coots are common.

Among the many wild flowers to

▲*The historic village of Old Brampton is one of the most attractive villages in the county. The little grebe (inset) makes its nest on a mound of water plants in still or gently flowing stretches of shallow water.*

FACT FILE

⁂ The Linacre Valley, 3 miles (4.8 km) west of Chesterfield off the B6050

▭ Pathfinder 761 (SK 36/37), grid reference SK 336728

miles 0 1 2 3 4 5 6 7 8 9 10 miles
kms 0 1 2 3 4 5 6 7 8 9 10 11 12 13 14 15 kms

◐ Allow 2½ hours

▬ Easy paths through woodland. Can be muddy in wet weather

P Car parks at the end of Barber Lane off the B6050; use the northernmost one

🍴 Pubs at Cutthorpe and Old Brampton; picnic area in Linacre Wood

LINACRE – OLD BRAMPTON

The walk begins from the car park at the end of Barber Lane.

1 Walk down the road to the next car park (on right). Look for the wooden stairway (very slippery when wet) at the edge of the car park and go down it into the wood. Turn right towards the middle reservoir **A** and continue along the track bordering its northern shore.

2 Walk on through the wood, keeping at the same level, and come to the eastern end of the upper reservoir **B**.

3 Bear right, then left after 50 yards (45 metres). Continue under the trees along the northern shore, crossing first one footbridge, then another at the upper end of the reservoir. Continue back along the southern shore to the southern end of the impounding wall.

4 Aim south-eastwards on path to the right of track along shore of reservoir. Proceed through the plantation to come out beside the southern shore of the middle reservoir and continue to the impounding wall. Bear left down the embankment to the foot of the Forty Steps **C** on the footpath leading to the right.

5 Climb the Forty Steps and cross the pasture in front. Old Brampton church **D** lies straight ahead. Climb a stile into North Lane, turn right and follow lane into the village of Brampton **E**.

6 Turn left at the telephone box, continuing

down the road to the church. Brampton Hall **F** is opposite.

7 At the far, north-eastern corner there is a footpath that crosses three fields to the impounding wall of the lower reservoir **G**. Cross this and go up the steps to the lane. Turn left along the lane to return to the starting point — the car park at the end of Barber Lane.

be seen in season is a thriving colony of Himalayan balsam, introduced here in the mid-1970s. In the summer the flowers bloom on the south-east corner of the middle reservoir.

ANCIENT SETTLEMENT

The Forty Steps **C**, a local landmark, lead to North Lane and the historic village of Old Brampton **E** listed in the Domesday Survey as Brantune. The blunt-spired parish church **D** was rebuilt in the 13th century, but Norman work can still be seen in an outer wall near the south doorway. Inside is an effigy of Matilda de Caus dating from 1224, but the large wooden cross is more recent. It is made from timbers brought back

from Ypres Cathedral in France, which was destroyed during World War I. Perhaps the most remarkable feature of the church is the unique 63-minute clock on the tower, the result of a workman's inaccuracy many years ago.

◀ *The attractive lakeside and woodland by the banks of the upper reservoir.*

▼ *A winter scene across pastureland to the spire of Old Brampton Church.*

Old Brampton Hall **F** stands under tall trees opposite the church. Its low west wing contains medieval cruck (curved) timbers, which indicate that this fine house must have existed for at least five centuries. Heading north out of the village, the path branches right to the impounding wall (built to contain stray animals) of the lower reservoir **G**, then back past the picnic site to the start of the walk.

BOTH PHOTOS ROGER REDFERN

LATHKILL DALE

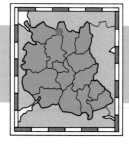

MIKE WILLIAMS

J WATKINS/FRANK LANE PICTURE AGENCY

A walk through one of Derbyshire's finest limestone dales

This is a classic walk through dramatic limestone scenery and wildlife habitats along one of the most beautiful dales in the White Peak district of Derbyshire.

Starting from the attractive hill village of Over Haddon, the greater part of the walk follows the crystal-clear, rushing waters of the River Lathkill as it flows on limestone through a National Nature Reserve,

FACT FILE

* Lathkill Dale, near Over Haddon, 3 miles (4.8 km) south of Bakewell, Derbyshire, just off the B5055 road

* Outdoor Leisure Map 24, grid reference SK 203674

miles 0 1 2 3 4 5 6 7 8 9 10 miles
kms 0 1 2 3 4 5 6 7 8 9 10 11 12 13 14 15 kms

* Allow 4 hours

* Moderately strenuous. Mostly good tracks and lanes. One long hill climb. Some sections by the river can become water-logged in very wet weather. Boots are recommended

* **P** Over Haddon — can get full on summer week-ends, Bank Holidays etc.

* Two small cafés in Over Haddon

* Pleasant pub at the very east end of the village, has superb views over the Dale

* **WC** Over Haddon car park

▲ *The waterfall at Tufa Dam provides a shady, damp habitat for ferns and mosses. The whitethroat (left) can be spotted in summer, especially in scrubby places, in the Peak District.*

which has particularly rich and varied flora and fauna. The return route is over quiet, rolling hill-farm land, providing many extensive views across the limestone hills and dales and over to the gritstone edges and moors that lie to the east.

LEAD VEIN

A short distance along the route old, ruined buildings are passed on the right of the path. These are the remains of an engine house built about 1840 to house a Cornish beam engine that pumped water from the Mandale Lead Mine **A**. A long vein of lead runs north-west from here. Known as the Mandale Rake it was worked from medieval times. The height of the mining activity was for a century between 1760 and 1860. The arched opening and water channel on the left of the path is the drainage level or 'south' from the mine. There is still an open, side

THE WALK

OVER HADDON – LATHKILL DALE

The walk starts from the car park in Over Haddon.

➊ From the car park in Over Haddon, turn right and follow the lane that leads steeply downhill into the Dale.

➋ Just before the ford, bear right through the two gates to continue on the track into Lathkill Dale with the river on your left-hand side. You are now entering the National Nature Reserve. This is a concessionary path. It can be closed very occasionally on some week days between the months of October and January. Permits are needed for large organized parties or if you wish to leave the path.

Follow this track for about 2 miles (3.2 km) past the Mandale Lead Mine Ⓐ, Palmerston Wood Ⓑ, Carter's Mill Ⓒ and the Tufa Dam Waterfall Ⓓ to reach a footbridge. If time permits, it is well worth continuing for another 300 yards (270 metres) up the Dale from this point to visit Lathkill Head Cave Ⓔ. Then retrace your steps back to the footbridge.

➌ Cross over the

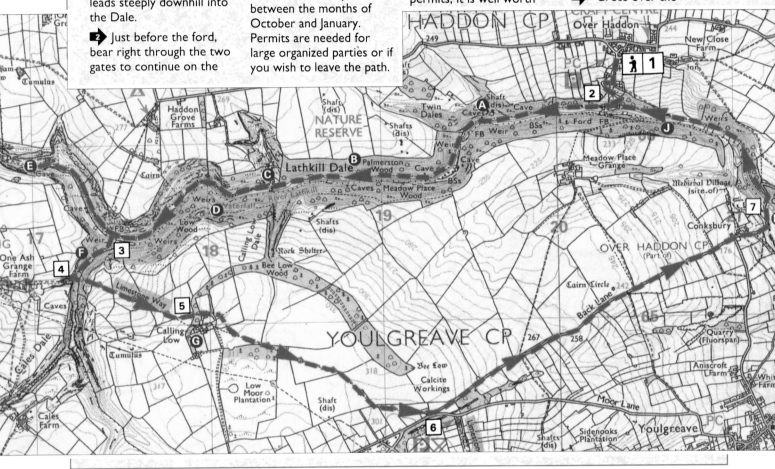

◀ *The remains of an old engine house at Mandale Lead Mine where lead has been worked since medieval times.*

entrance to the mine, which the miners used, but the workings are unstable and partially flooded and should on no account be entered.

Continuing you reach Palmerston Wood Ⓑ where more remains of mining activities can be seen. There are ruined buildings and spoil heaps, partly for lead, and also for chert, a mineral substance very much like flint. This is a good area to look for dogwood, guelder rose, hart's tongue fern and lily of the valley at the appropriate seasons throughout the year.

Carrying on alongside the river you reach Carter's Mill Ⓒ. Only the foundation stones can now be seen of the early 19th-century mill that ground corn brought down from Over Haddon. Two millstones can still be seen lying half buried nearby. The weirs and dams remain intact though and the mill pond behind is a good spot to find water plants such as water crowfoot. This is a good habitat for moorhens, mallards and little grebes, the latter often nesting on floating platforms of reeds in the middle of the pool.

A little further on you approach the Tufa Dam Waterfall Ⓓ. In wet weather there is a fine waterfall here. In dry weather conditions, the

footbridge and follow the path into Cales Dale **F** for about 200 yards (180 metres). Where the path forks, take the left-hand path down to stile.

4 Cross over the stile and ascend the stepped path ahead to reach a kissing gate. Follow the clearly defined path ahead,

across the fields to Calling Low farm **G**. At this stage look back and enjoy the wonderful views.

5 Follow the diverted path around the left-hand side of the farm. Continue on the well-defined path across the fields, through the corner of the wood, to reach the lane.

6 There is an attractive picnic site 150 yards (135 metres) down the right forking lane, with a fine viewpoint. To continue the walk through, turn left on reaching main lane and follow it for 1 mile (1.6 km) downhill to Conksbury Bridge **H**.

7 Cross over the bridge

and turn left through the gate onto the track which follows the river **J** back to the ford near Over Haddon. This lane is narrow with small verges and sharp corners so extreme care should be taken. Turn right back up the hill to return to your start at the car park.

▼ *Carter's Mill has been used to grind corn since the early 1800s. The pool is an excellent habitat for nesting birds.*

river often flows underground here and farther up the dale and springs bubble up at this point. This is a natural waterfall, unlike the weirs lower down the river. It is of unusual interest to geologists as it is not formed from the limestone rock, but is composed of tufa, a complex build-up of mineral deposits formed from calcium carbonate. This waterfall is a favourite haunt for dippers, which nest under the over-hanging rocks.

Shortly further on it is worth taking a 300-yard (270-metre) diversion to look at Lathkill Dale Head Cave **E**. This is the site of the river's resurgence in wet weather, when a great torrent of water pours out from underground streams.

Although wide and high at the entrance, the cave soon narrows and lowers, although it extends back through more than 1,000 feet (305 metres) of passages, but this is strictly the domain of experienced cavers and pot-holers.

SHEEP-WASH

Returning to the main route you come to three smaller caves in this valley, the lowest one again containing an underground stream in wet weather. Remains of lynx were found in the upper caves. This spot is known as Cales Dale **F**. For centuries, sheep were brought down the dale to a sheep wash by the river, where fleeces were washed prior to shearing. The ruined wall enclosures of the sheep folds and

pens can still be seen today in the area near the footbridge.

Leaving the river and walking on the Limestone Way you pass Calling Low Farm **G**, a typical, fine, large Derbyshire hill farm, which was once a monastic estate. In the wood nearby is an Iron Age burial mound known as Bee Low.

The river is rejoined at Conksbury **H**, originally the site of a large, medieval, monastic settlement, where earth works can still be seen in the field on the left bank of the river near the bridge. This probably explains why the fairly rare herbal plant green hellebore

▼ *Lathkill Head Cave is the primary source of the River Lathkill. Generally it is dry in summer and wet in winter.*

ALL PHOTOS MIKE WILLIAMS

has been found in the Dale nearby, as it was used in medieval times as a medicinal herb.

The last stretch of the walk includes a particularly attractive section of the river that is sometimes known as the Blue Waters ❶ and has long been a famous spot for angling. It is one of the best places to observe the many water fowl — mallards, little grebe, moorhens. The deeper

▲ *The serene beauty of the route along the lane to Conksbury bridge offers fine, panoramic views across Peak uplands.*

pools are sometimes stocked with brown trout and grayling and this attracts the occasional marauding heron. Water voles also frequent the reed beds, and the river banks here are another good site for the many marsh plants, especially butterbur and marsh ragwort.

The woods in the Nature Reserve are composed predominantly of ash and elm trees. The elms are suffering from Dutch elm disease and could soon disappear. The ancient, native

Lathkill Dale Nature Reserve

The Reserve was the first one to be established in the Peak District National Park, and now covers most of the Dale along both sides of the river. It is managed by the Nature Conservancy Council. Permits are needed for large, organized groups, or if you wish to leave the concessionary paths or marked public rights-of-way.

The reserve contains one of the country's purest rivers, the Lathkill, which is unique in that it rises and flows entirely on limestone. The ancient ash woodlands go back to pre-Norman times and have been remarkably undisturbed by man. These features have combined to provide an area of particularly rich and varied flora and fauna.

The valley is heavily wooded in the lower sections, mainly with hawthorn, alder, ash and crack willow. Sadly, many of the trees have suffered considerable damage in recent years from severe winter gales, heavy snowfalls, exceptionally dry summers and Dutch elm disease.

The extensive woodland provides good cover for many smaller birds — finches, tits and warblers in the spring and summer. The river is a great haunt for dippers, especially near the larger waterfalls. On the deeper, calmer pools, look out for water hens, mallard, little grebe and wagtails. Jackdaws frequent the higher limestone crags.

There is a particularly rich variety of flora, especially river and marsh plants, such as marsh ragwort, water parsnip, butterbur and fool's water cress. On the damp, rocky sides of the river path dogwood, guelder rose, lily of the valley and yellow archangel can all be found. Higher up on the stony slopes rockrose and wild thyme grow.

The river used to be well stocked with brown trout and grayling, but now these can only be found in the deeper, lower pools. Problems as a result of drought and visitor pressure have led to a considerable decline in fishing activities on the river. Water voles though are still common and can often be seen in the day time, especially in the deeper pools and near the reed beds.

The butterbur flower, which favours damp ground, is one example of the profusion of flora to be found in Lathkill Dale.

◀*Lathkill Dale is one of Derbyshire's finest limestone dales with one of the country's purest rivers running through.*

ash woods make a special contribution to providing habitat for wildlife. Ash trees come into leaf late and when in leaf provide only a light shade. Also the leaves decompose quickly once they fall. The combination of these factors means a rich variety of plant life can flourish on the woodland floor. Among the species to be seen in this environment are dog's mercury, hazel and yellow archangel, the latter indicating ancient woodland.

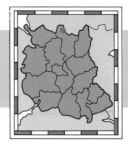
DERBYSHIRE

MIKE WILLIAMS. INSET: PEKKA HELO/BRUCE COLEMAN LTD

FACT FILE

* Ladybower Reservoir, 12 miles (19km) west of Sheffield

* Outdoor Leisure Map 1, grid reference SK 173893

  miles 0 1 2 3 4 5 6 7 8 9 10 miles
  kms 0 1 2 3 4 5 6 7 8 9 10 11 12 13 14 15 kms

* Allow 4 to 5 hours

* A strenuous hill walk, with some long, steep ascents and descents. Not suitable for young children or the elderly. The moors can be boggy — boots are essential. Be prepared for bad weather

* **P** Fairholmes car park at start of walk

* Picnic site and café (open only in summer) at car park

* **WC** At car park

* **I** Access to the moors is occasionally restricted during the grouse shooting season (12 August to 10 December); Tel. (01629) 814321 or (01433) 670216 for details

▲ *The fortress-like Derwent Dam, built before the end of World War I, was the scene of World War II manoeuvres. Cloudberries (left) grow on the wild moorland that overlooks it.*

Grouse moors, tors and reservoirs in the Dark Peak area

This walk explores the challenging hill country and man-made lakes of the Peak District, on the border between Yorkshire and Derbyshire. It begins in the shadow of the Derwent Dam **A**, scene of wartime practice flights by 'The Dambusters'. The dam, 115 feet (35m) high, can look particularly spectacular when surplus water from the Derwent Reservoir cascades over it. It is also impressive when it ices over in severe winters.

The route leads north past the dam and through Hancock Wood **B** along the east bank of the reservoir.

Most of the hillsides surrounding the reservoirs have been extensively planted with conifers. There is a continual cycle of felling and replanting, with most of the timber being used for fence posts and planks. At lower levels, however, you pass between tracts of deciduous woodland where there are sycamore, beech and oak trees.

DENSE WOODLAND

The dense (and consequently dark) conifer plantations are not rich in their variety of wildlife, but coal tits and goldcrests can be seen, as well as the occasional goshawk. Grey wagtails and dippers can sometimes be found at points where streams flow into the reservoirs.

A steep climb up through the woods brings you out onto the wild expanse of Howden Moors, where there is a good covering of heather as well as cotton grass. Bilberry, cloudberry and crowberry also grow

THE WALK

LADYBOWER RESERVOIR – DERWENT EDGE

The walk begins at the National Park Information Centre car park at Fairholmes, 2 miles (3.2km) up the Derwent Valley road from the A57 Manchester-Sheffield road.

1 Take the path leading to the road at the base of Derwent Dam **A**. Turn right onto the road and follow it to a junction with a gravel track.

2 Ignoring the gravel track, take the path on your left to ascend through the plantation and past the top of the dam. Cross a stile to a broad track. After walking alongside the reservoir for ½ mile (800m), you come to a public footpath, signposted to Bradfield and Strines.

3 Follow this path, ascending steeply through Hancock Wood **B**. Continue up onto the moors along the waymarked path, to reach a footpath signpost near a ruined wall.

4 Bear right to follow the footpath. Follow the wall round, bearing right, then cross a large stile over a fence. Follow the main footpath across the moor towards Derwent Edge. Take care, especially in misty or bad weather conditions, to avoid a track that runs parallel for a while, but eventually splits off to the left. Continue to the crest of the Edge.

5 At a signpost about 200 yards (180m) south of the trig point on Back Tor, turn right and follow the broad path along Derwent Edge, passing the Cakes of Bread rock formation **C**, Dovestone Tor, the Salt Cellar **D** and White Tor.

6 About 100 yards (90m) beyond White Tor, turn right down a small path. (If you reach a signpost and path crossroads you have gone too far.) Follow the small path steeply down through heather and bracken to reach a footpath signpost by a wall. Continue down past a plantation and Grindle Clough to reach a track running alongside Ladybower Reservoir.

7 Turn right along the track, past the drowned village of Derwent **E** on your left. This track becomes a road and leads back to the start.

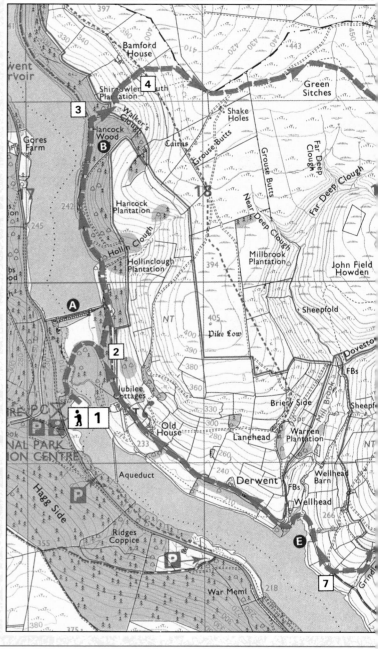

here, though less profusely. The moors look particularly splendid in early autumn, when the purple heather is in full bloom.

WHITE HARE

These are traditionally grouse moors, and plenty of red grouse can still be seen, although their numbers have declined in recent years. Curlews and golden plovers are also in evidence, as well as kestrels, soaring and hovering along the gritstone

◀ *Where the route passes through Hancock Wood there are some fine vistas over the Derwent Reservoir.*

edges. The mountain hare, whose coat turns white in the winter months, is one of the more interesting mammals to be found here.

RUGGED ROCKS

Just below Back Tor, the route turns south along the ridge of Derwent Edge, which provides superb views on all sides. The craggy edges and gritstone tors (hills) are the last remnants of hard sedimentary rocks formed millions of years ago in shallow, tropical seas.

They have been eroded by the Ice Ages, and subsequently weathered by wind, rain, snow and ice into

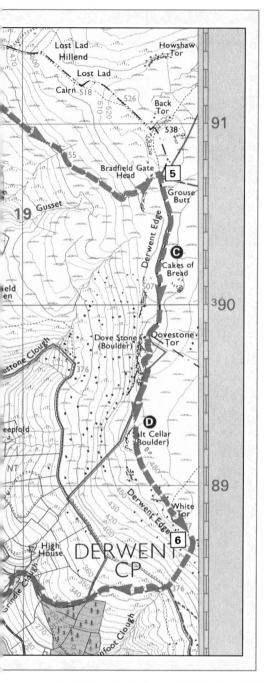

▲*Beyond Hancock Wood, the path climbs up onto the moors. From Derwent Edge (right), literally the high point of the walk, there are magnificent views over the surrounding countryside.*

their present strange and fantastic shapes. The gritstone was frequently quarried for millstones as well as local building stone.

CAKES OF BREAD

Over the years, the tors have acquired names to match their curious features — Cakes of Bread **C** and the Salt Cellar **D** are particularly easy to recognize. Just beyond White Tor, the route takes you steeply down through the pretty

▼*The triangulation point on Derwent Edge's Back Tor records its height of 1,765 feet (538m) above sea level.*

little valley of Grindle Clough towards Ladybower Reservoir.

When the Bamford Dam was built, and the level of the reservoir began to rise to a level greater than anticipated, the village of Derwent **E** became submerged, along with much of the lower Derwent Valley. The cottages, farms, school, church and vicarage became unsafe and all had to be demolished in 1943. The bodies from the graveyard were reburied at Bamford, and the residents of Derwent were rehoused at nearby Yorkshire Bridge.

Derwent Lodge, a shooting lodge owned by successive Dukes of Norfolk, but used as a youth hostel just before World War II, also had to be demolished. For a time, the church spire could be seen rising above the water, but in 1947 it was

► *Along Derwent Edge are some curious rock formations that bear names to match. This boulder is the Salt Cellar.*

BOTH PHOTOS: MIKE WILLIAMS

The Dams and Reservoirs

Ladybower, Derwent and Howden Reservoirs, linked by dams, provide over 42 million gallons (200 million litres) of water a day, mainly for the cities of Sheffield, Nottingham, Derby and Leicester. The two massive stone dams of Derwent and Howden, which lies further up the valley, were built between 1902 and 1916 of gritstone quarried some distance away and transported up the valley by a specially built railway line. Traces of the line can still be seen here and there along the sides of the reservoirs.

The demand for water for the industrial area of the north Midlands increased steadily. A third dam was built at Bamford between 1935 and 1945, creating the Ladybower Reservoir, opened by George VI, and

flooding the Lower Ashop and Derwent valleys. The little villages of Derwent and Ashopton were accidentally flooded in the process.

In 1943, the Howden and Derwent dams and reservoirs were used by the RAF for secret tests and low-level practice flights. Lancaster bombers of 617 Squadron, better known as 'The Dambusters', flew up and down here in preparation for their raids on dams in the Ruhr Valley, and again when the well-known film was made. In May 1988, the last remaining Lancaster of the squadron made a memorial flight over the Derwent Dam.

At the turn of the century, Derwent was a pretty village with a thriving community. Today, it lies at the bottom of a reservoir.

PEAK NATIONAL PARK

▼*When the water level of Ladybower Reservoir is low, it is possible to see the sad remains of Derwent village.*

considered unsafe and pulled down. The village's fine old packhorse bridge was rebuilt at Slippery Stones. In times of extreme drought, the water level of the reservoir drops considerably, revealing sad glimpses of the former village's buildings, walls and lanes.

The last section of the walk takes you along the bank of Ladybower Reservoir. Finally, you rejoin your original path past Derwent Dam and return to the car park.

DERBYSHIRE

A walk through parks and farmland to three great houses

This walk begins and ends in Melbourne, a pleasant South Derbyshire town of mellow, red-brick buildings, and passes through varied farm, park and woodland scenery. There are opportunities to visit two unusual churches and fine old houses and gardens at Melbourne, Staunton Harold and Calke. Along the way, there are glorious views of the Staunton Harold Reservoir, a scenic modern addition to this varied landscape.

Melbourne, where the walk begins, is a centre for market gardening on the rich, dark, loam soils of the surrounding region. There are several timber-framed houses, including a cruck-house in the High Street, and some Georgian and Victorian shop-fronts.

VICTORIAN ALMSHOUSES

Thomas Cook, the travel agent, was born in Melbourne in 1808, and his name is perpetuated by the Cook Almshouses in the High Street, built in 1890. They are administered by a charitable trust he set up.

FACT FILE

- Melbourne, 6 miles (9.6km) south of Derby

- Pathfinder 852 (SK 22/32), grid reference SK 389249

  miles 0 1 2 3 4 5 6 7 8 9 10 miles
  kms 0 1 2 3 4 5 6 7 8 9 10 11 12 13 14 15 kms

- Allow at least 4 hours

- Mainly undulating field paths, which can be steep. Muddy after rain and overgrown in summer. Numerous stiles and the occasional fence to climb

- **P** Opposite the church at the start

- **T** Buses to Melbourne from Derby

- Pubs in Melbourne. Melbourne Craft Centre tea-rooms, Staunton Harold Hall coffee shop, Calke Abbey cafeteria

- **I** For opening times of Melbourne Hall, its craft centre and gardens, Staunton Harold's church, Staunton Stables Craft Centre, and Calke Abbey (National Trust), Tel. (01332) 255802. Calke Park is open all year in daylight hours

▲ *Across Melbourne Pool, at the southern edge of town, there are views back to the parish church and Melbourne Hall. Harebells (inset) grow in local meadows and on the verges.*

The Church of St Michael with St Mary **Ⓐ** is one of the most splendid Norman churches in England. It was built around 1120, possibly as a royal chapel for Henry I, and has been little altered. The massive pillars of the nave arcade are particularly impressive, as is the chevron moulding on the doorways and arches. There are some interesting carvings on the capitals in the chancel, including a grinning cat, a snarling dog and an ostrich.

Opposite the main door, to the right of the vicarage, a plaque marks the site of the Old Smithy, where Robert Bakewell, the celebrated ironsmith, set up his forge in 1707.

MELBOURNE HALL

Not far away is Melbourne Hall **Ⓑ**. It is privately owned, but well worth a visit in its open season. There are delightful rooms, with pictures and furnishings from the 17th and 18th centuries. In 1837, a tiny settlement on the banks of the Yarra-Yarra in Australia was named 'Melbourne' after the 2nd Lord Melbourne, who

THE WALK

MELBOURNE – STAUNTON HAROLD – CALKE

The walk begins at Melbourne's parish church **A**, *in Pool Road.*

1 Walk through the large gateway by the church. Follow the road around the lake, past Melbourne Hall and gardens **B**.

2 Where the lane swings away from the lake at an overflow, take the second right footpath, signposted for Burney Lane. Follow the footpath across two fields, and alongside a wood in the third. Leaving the wood, the path dips. Climb the stile at the bottom of the dip and follow the line of trees up to a gate. Follow the path between two lines of trees. Continue ahead along the edge of the coppice and through the next field, heading towards a large horse chestnut tree in the dip. Climb a stile by the tree, then another and take a path left, uphill, at a footpath sign. At the top, climb a stile by a hedge and a footpath sign, and walk across the field to a lane.

3 Turn right towards a new bungalow and continue to the junction with the B587. Turn left and continue uphill. Just past a wood, turn right down the lane to Staunton Harold Hall **C** and church **D**. Continue on the lane, up past Staunton Stables Craft Centre, then down towards a small stream. Just before a stream, take the grassy footpath right, and follow the hedge. Climb a stile to continue ahead through a wood.

4 The public footpath is crossed by a fairly high, but easily climbed fence that

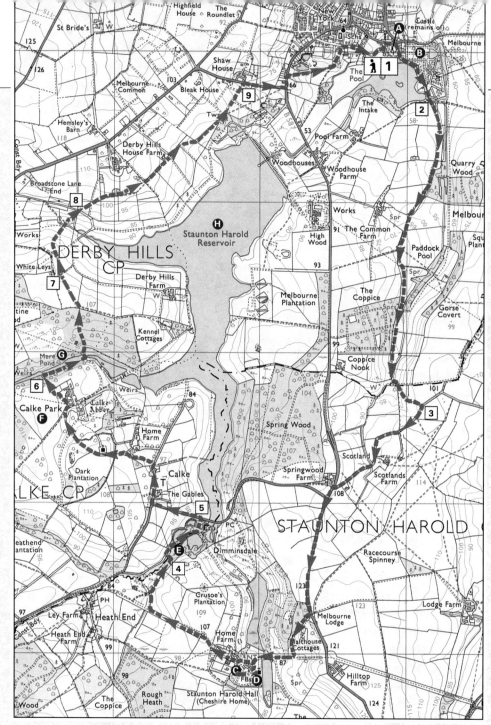

marks the boundary of the Dimminsdale nature reserve **E**. About 50 paces beyond the fence, take the path left down to the stream and cross the footbridge. Climb the path up to the fence and follow it right. Follow the path through the nature reserve, past the ponds and up some steps to your left. Go past the limekilns and information board, and on to the exit.

5 Walk left up the road to a junction. Turn right down the lane signposted

to Calke village. After a thatched white cottage, turn left on the road into Calke Park **F**. Follow it past the church to the main house entrance. Continue ahead past the stables and walled car park. Follow the fence of the overspill car park/picnic area towards some trees. Continue ahead, being sure to keep to the left side of the fence. Go down some steps to Mere Pond **G**.

6 Bear right along the bank. Go left round the end of the pond, and

continue on the path uphill. Keep to the fence, ignoring left turns. At the top, the path swings left in front of a stone wall. After about 25 paces, go through a gate in the wall on your right. The path continues left, then after a few paces is waymarked to the right, across a field and down towards a house, White Leys.

7 Just before White Leys, the path crosses a lane. Continue ahead, close by the house and uphill. As you descend again, look

Nature Walk

Sophisticated machines harvest fruit and vegetables that are grown on a large scale. Look out for:

POTATO HARVESTERS Men working on the machines remove any stones before bagging the potatoes.

PEA HARVESTERS These cut the crop, shell the peas and empty them into containers ready for processing.

RICHARD PHIPPS

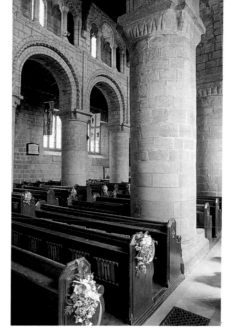

▲*The Church of St Michael with St Mary has some impressive drum pillars and decorated Norman arches.*

and 'Harold' after a 12th-century lord of the manor. The village has long since disappeared. All that remains are the hall and the church, facing each other in a picturesque wooded valley with a lake.

PALLADIAN MANOR

The manor came to the Shirley family by marriage in 1423. The present hall **C**, begun in 1763 by Washington Shirley, the 5th Earl of Ferrers, is not open to the public. It is used as a Cheshire Home for the disabled. However, there are pleasant strolls to be had around the grounds. In the farm buildings above the hall, the Staunton Stables Craft Centre houses traditional craft shops round a magnificent Georgian courtyard.

Staunton Harold's church **D** was founded during the Commonwealth by Sir Robert Shirley, an ardent Royalist. Shirley soon fell foul of Cromwell, and died in the Tower, but the church survived. Gothic in its architecture and Jacobean in its furniture and fittings, it has many interesting features, including a carved tablet to the memory of Sir

lived in the hall. Well known as Queen Victoria's first prime minister, Lord Melbourne was also the husband of Lady Caroline Lamb, the most daring and scandalous woman of the age. She had a disastrous affair with Lord Byron, whom she pursued relentlessly, even attempting suicide to capture his affection.

The formal garden is one of the most famous in Britain. Designed by Thomas Coke in the 17th century it was ambitiously planned 'to suit with Versailles'. Although not large, it contains, among other delights, a 'Four Seasons' monument that was reputedly the gift of Queen Anne, the longest yew tunnel in Europe, a lime walk and a formal pool, across which stands Robert Bakewell's magical wrought-iron birdcage.

The route passes through the gates on Pool Road. On the right is Melbourne Pool, an attractive artificial lake enlarged from a medieval millpond in the 18th century.

You continue across mixed farmland and woodland and rejoin the road near Scotlands Farm, over the border into Leicestershire. Views of the countryside to the east are dominated by the church of Breedon on the Hill on its lonely crag.

By Melbourne Lodge, a path descends from the road to Staunton Harold — 'Staunton' after a local name for the limestone hereabouts,

BOTH PHOTOS: ROBERT EAMES

▲*Behind this imposing gateway is the red-brick Staunton Harold Hall, a large building in the Palladian style.*

carefully for the waymark sign at a path junction by a large tree. Take the right-hand path and go down across the field to the valley bottom. Climb a stile and cross the plank bridge over the stream, then take the path uphill ahead.

8 At the top of the hill, cross a lane and a

signposted stile. Continue ahead along a well defined footpath across seven fields, with Staunton Harold Reservoir **H** on your right. At the eighth field, the path continues towards the lookout tower ahead. Go past the tower, but do not climb the stile into the amenity

area; instead, continue along the path, which drops down to join a road opposite Shaw House.

9 Turn right, then left at the Melbourne Arms. After about 100 yards (90m), cross the road and go through a kissing-gate. Take the path downhill and across the fields by the

wall and fence to the houses of Melbourne. Turn right along a road and continue ahead; go past the vehicle 'no entry' signs at the junction with Salisbury Lane. At the end of Penn Lane, turn right into Church Street, then first right into Pool Road to return to the start.

◄*Calke Abbey, the third great house on the route, is now a National Trust property and is open to the public.*

Robert over the west door. The painted wooden ceiling, showing the Creation, is signed by Zachary and Samuel Kyrk and dated 1655.

The hangings and cushions are contemporary, as are the organ and the early wood-framed clock. The splendid, wrought-iron chancel grille was made by Robert Bakewell in 1711. The 17th-century custom of separating the men into the southern pews (with hat-pegs) and the women into the northern pews, is still observed in this church today.

A country lane takes you through Dimminsdale **E**, an attractive nature reserve (see box) set in a wooded valley with an interesting industrial past. On a hot day, the woods provide welcome shade and coolness.

Beyond is Calke Abbey **F**, an 18th-century mansion set in parkland on the site of an Augustinian priory. Largely unchanged for the past 100 years, it was restored by public appeal and the National Trust in the 1980s and was then opened to the public for the first time.

BUTTERFLY COLLECTION

It was the seat of the Harpur-Crewe family, who had a colourful history. A number of them were decidedly reclusive and eccentric, and several were passionate collectors. Sir Vauncey Harpur-Crewe (1846-1924) devoted himself to his passions for butterflies, birds and hunting. His large and exotic collection is now on view to visitors. The gardens, too, are interesting, though not yet fully restored. There are fine views of the mansion as the walk passes through superb rolling parkland on the way to the tranquil Mere Pond **G**, a haven for waterfowl.

The final part of the walk is through undulating farmland, with views of Staunton Harold Reservoir **H** to the right, before you descend through tranquil meadows to the quiet back streets of Melbourne, which take you back to the start.

▼*This cruck-house in Melbourne has intriguing brickwork and timbering.*

Around Dimminsdale

Several ponds on the reserve provide a protected habitat for aquatic plants, dragonflies, waterbirds and fish.

Dimminsdale, at the southern end of Staunton Harold Reservoir, is owned by Severn-Trent Water, and leased to the Leicestershire and Rutland Trust for Nature Conservation as a nature reserve. A Site of Special Scientific Interest, its mixture of soil types, woods and ponds provides varied habitats for a number of birds and plants not often found together. Look for primroses in spring and hart's tongue ferns in summer. You may see a speckled wood butterfly, and perhaps even a kingfisher.

The secluded ponds are water-filled quarry workings. From the 13th century onwards, limestone and other minerals were excavated here. The remains of kilns, where the stone was burned to produce lime, are still visible, and others are submerged in the ponds.

One Dimminsdale quarry was owned by the Harpur-Crewe estate of Calke, and another, now known as the Laundry Pool, was quarried by the Earls of Ferrers, who lived at Staunton Harold. The pool takes its name from a cottage that once stood here and was used as a laundry by Staunton Harold Hall.

The path through the reserve follows the course of an old tramway, a branch of a primitive, horse-drawn line that was created in 1802, in the canal age, and survived long into the railway age. It ran for 8 miles (12.8km) through rural Leicestershire and South Derbyshire, connecting the lime workings of the Ticknall area with the Willesley Canal, south of Ashby. The tramroad was laid with cast-iron rails, 25 years before George Stephenson built the Stockton and Darlington Railway, and Ticknall is widely known for its place in transport history.

The 'Dimsdale' branch of the tramway opened in 1830. In 1845, the Midland Railway Company bought it and turned the main tramroad into a standard gauge railway. All that remained of the horse-drawn traffic was the Ticknall and Dimsdale lines. The Dimsdale branch continued in use until 1891, and the last trip over the Ticknall line is believed to have been in 1913.

near the church. The hall was demolished in the 1930s.

You pass the village pond, which is lively with ducks and attractively overgrown with water plants. At a crossroads stands Doveridge Well, a handsome focal point. Now capped over, it was once an essential part of village life. By the post office are the village stocks, complete with a wooden seat for comfort.

ELIZABETHAN HALL

Somersal Herbert takes its name from the FitzHerbert family, lords of the manor in the 13th century. The hamlet nestles in a hollow among the fields. Approaching the hall **B** from the south, you see it as a modern brick mansion. As you walk round towards the church, a gateway reveals that the north front is a half-timbered Elizabethan hall.

The effect is quite delightful. There is an assortment of gables, timber motifs and wood-mullioned windows, and the whole front is framed by 18th-century gate-piers capped with urns. The hall, built in

◀ *The half-timbered, Elizabethan north front of the hall at Somersal Herbert can be glimpsed from the road. Lawyer's wig (inset), an edible fungus, grows in damp grass nearby.*

A Tudor mansion set amid the rich pasture of the lovely Dove Valley

Quiet and charming, the village of Doveridge rises above the lush watermeadows of the River Dove. A walk across the fields leads to the romantic hamlet of Somersal Herbert and an outstanding gem of Elizabethan architecture.

The starting point is St Cuthbert's Church **A**, the dedication of which suggests there was a pre-Norman settlement here; Cuthbert was a popular Anglo-Saxon saint. There is a magnificent view across the Dove

Valley from the churchyard, which is dominated by a mighty yew, between 1,200 and 1,400 years old, its spreading branches secured by a labyrinth of props. According to local legend, Robin Hood and Maid Marian were betrothed beneath these boughs. There is a stone cross with a 13th-century base; the top sections were added to honour the victims of World War I.

The resident bat population has left its mark on the floors of the church. The building has a very wide nave and chancel with no arch between them, increasing the air of space. There are good memorials to members of the Cavendish family, who lived in an 18th-century hall

FACT FILE

* Doveridge, 2 miles (3.2km) east of Uttoxeter, on the A50

* Pathfinder 831 (SK 03/13), grid reference SK 114341

  miles 0 1 2 3 4 5 6 7 8 9 10 miles
  kms 0 1 2 3 4 5 6 7 8 9 10 11 12 13 14 15 kms

* Allow 3 hours

* Mainly level walking, but some overgrown paths can be wet and muddy after rain. One steep scramble

* **P** In the streets of Doveridge, and space for several cars near church

* The Cavendish Arms in Doveridge

1564, is not open to the public.

Next door is the Church of St Peter **C**, rebuilt in 1874. It contains a Norman font, and a memorial to John FitzHerbert and his wife Mary, dated 1601. The tapering cross in the churchyard is even older than the hall. It stands on three steps and is reached by a path lined with roses.

The route returns to the River

▶ *As the route makes its final return to Doveridge, it crosses the Dove on this nicely proportioned suspension bridge.*

Dove, here a mature river making its final approach to the Trent. The lovely, six-arched, stone bridge **D** was built in 1691. From it, with your back to the A50, you can see the misty, distant Derbyshire hills.

On the return to Doveridge, you cross a remarkable suspension bridge **E**, the only one still in use in Derbyshire. The length of its span causes it to spring considerably as weight moves across it — quite an experience when the Dove is in full flood beneath!

THE WALK

DOVERIDGE – SOMERSAL HERBERT

*The walk starts at St Cuthbert's Church **A**, Doveridge.*

1 Walk back along Church Lane. Follow the High Street into the village. Go over the crossroads to Bakers Lane and turn left. Cross the A50. Do not climb the stile, but take the waymarked grassy path to the right. Go over a stile, and walk along the right edge of two fields. From the end of the second field,

continue ahead on the waymarked path on the other side of the hedge to Brocksford Brook.

2 Cross a footbridge. The relatively indistinct path goes uphill to the right of Mill Farm ahead. Skirt all the buildings and continue, with the fence on your left, to Grove Lane. Leave the field by a wooden gate to your left, then a metal gate into the lane.

3 Turn left and go past Mill Farm to Somersal Herbert. Turn left at the junction, and walk past the hall **B** to St Peter's Church **C**. Just beyond the churchyard, take the signposted footpath left across the middle of the field, keeping left of the oak trees. Make for a stile near

a wooded depression. Continue ahead across the next field, heading for a line of three large oaks. Pass to the left of the right-hand one and continue ahead to a waymarked footbridge.

4 Cross and head for the top left-hand corner of the next field. Climb the stile and follow a cart track ahead, past Field Farm on your left. Continue on the path alongside the farm drive, to a lane. Turn left and continue to the A50.

5 Turn right, then immediately right again into Upwoods Road. Fork left at North Lodge. The road eventually crosses a cattle grid and becomes a public bridleway. At the overhead sign for the Dove Sporting Club, the Staffordshire

Way crosses the bridleway.

6 Turn left. Follow the Staffordshire Way along the right-hand field edges. Where the path descends sharply to the river, make for the stone bridge **D**.

7 Climb the stile to the left of the bridge, and take the path through the trees. There is a steep scramble up to the bridge. Cross, and cut through the trees on your left to reach the main road-bridge. Cross the road carefully, and look for a stile down to the right bank of the River Dove. Walk along the raised bank ahead, across the meadow. Cross the suspension bridge **E** and continue to the lane. Turn right up the hill to return to St Cuthbert's Church.

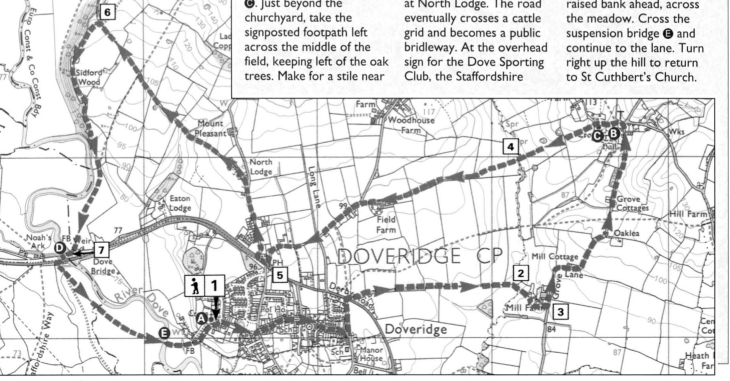

SHERWOOD FOREST

A woodland and river walk in the heart of Robin Hood country

The legend of Robin Hood and his Merry Men is one of the most endearing stories in English folklore. This walk follows paths through the fabled forest of oak to see many places associated with him — the Major Oak, the Centre Tree, and one of the many churches where he is reputed to have married Maid Marian.

The first half of the walk leads through woodland and the second goes through more open country beside a river and past an impressive 19th-century lodge where statues of Robin Hood and Maid Marian can be seen. There is an interesting difference in plant and bird life in the two types of landscape, and a further contrast on the return leg of the walk through the village of Edwinstowe.

The walk starts from the Visitors' Centre of the Sherwood Forest Country Park **Ⓐ**. The country park covers 450 acres (182 hectares),

FACT FILE

✳ Edwinstowe, Sherwood Forest, 2 miles (3 km) west of Ollerton on A6075

▭ Pathfinder 780 (SK 66/76), grid reference SK 626675

miles 0 1 2 3 4 5 6 7 8 9 10 miles
kms 0 1 2 3 4 5 6 7 8 9 10 11 12 13 14 15 kms

◔ Allow 2½ hours

▬ Well-defined tracks and paths throughout. Can be wet in winter and walking boots are advised

Ⓟ Sherwood Forest Visitors' Centre, beside the B6034

🍴 Refreshments at car park. Shops, restaurants and inns in Edwinstowe

WC At car park

▲ *Although a fraction of its former size, the forest still retains a magical feel, making it one of the most beautiful places for walks in the country. (inset) A leghorn beetle basks in the sunshine.*
▶ *The Major Oak, the largest tree in England, has been spreading its boughs for hundreds of years.*

almost all that is left of Sherwood Forest. Originally it was a royal hunting forest which covered a fifth of the county of Nottinghamshire. Famed for its many ancient oak trees, the park is now a Site of Special Scientific Interest because of these and its other flora and fauna. The centre has a permanent exhibition on the legend of Robin Hood and Sherwood Forest, a gift shop and Robin Hood's Larder for food.

MAJOR ATTRACTION

The Major Oak **Ⓑ** is the largest tree in the forest, and the largest oak tree in England, and is now heavily propped by timber supports. This hollow tree is a very popular tourist attraction, being one of the supposed meeting and hiding places for Robin Hood and his men. Originally it was known as the Queen's Oak but became known as the Major Oak after Major Hayman

THE WALK

EDWINSTOWE

The walk begins at the Sherwood Forest Visitors' Centre **A** *and takes an anti-clockwise direction.*

1 Follow the signs to The Major Oak **B**. The well-defined path starts on the immediate left of the entrance to the Visitors' Centre and is fenced most of the way. It is ½ mile (800 metres) along the track to the tree, with blue-topped posts marking the route along the way.

2 Continue along the track round the tree and take the first left track beyond it. Follow this well-made track for about 350 yards (315 metres).

3 At the track junction turn right (not sharp right) and follow the defined track indicated by the large green and white arrowed bridleway sign, a feature of this woodland section. Pass a similar sign in 300 yards (270 metres) and keep on this track for another ½ mile (800 metres) to the next track junction.

4 Bear left and follow the often grass-covered track, crossing a similar track after a few yards, for little over ¼ mile

Bracket fungus is just one of the species of flora and fauna that make the forest a delight for nature lovers.

Rooke, a local antiquary, who lived nearby in Mansfield Woodhouse in the 18th century. Another name for it is the Cock Pen Oak, as cock fighting took place under it.

The tree's hollow can hold many people and on one occasion 30 suffragettes managed to squeeze in. The tree measures 40 feet (12 metres) around the base of its trunk and its widest boughs cover a circle of 260 feet (78 metres) in circumference. The hollow cavity measures 7 feet (2.1 metres) in diameter and 15 feet (4.5 metres) high. Another tree was known as Robin Hood's Larder where he is reputed to have stored his food and venison. Sadly, this tree has now disappeared.

TREES OF THE FOREST

While the forest is renowned for its oak trees (in 1609 it was on record that there were 21,000 of them in Birklands) many are just shells, often referred to as stag-headed oaks. There are also considerable expanses of birch — known locally as the Lady of the Wood — syca-more, sweet chestnut and pine. In

(400 metres) to a track junction and a wooden bar across the track.

5 Turn left, heading due south, and follow a well-defined track, signed as a bridleway, for ¾ mile (1200 metres) to the oak Centre Tree.

6 Carry straight on following the bridleway sign and take the path a little to the right of a pine plantation for almost ¾ mile (1200 metres) to the A6075 road. Just before the road, the path bears right to a track.

7 Cross the track and follow a path just inside the wood to avoid walking on the road. Continue for 250 yards (225 metres) until it turns left to the main road (A6075).

8 Cross the A6075 road to the gravel track and signed bridleway. Follow the track round to the right and after ¼ mile (400 metres) pass Archway Lodge **C** on the left. Just after this descend the track to a bridge over the River Maun.

9 Turn left just before the bridge and following the bridleway signpost take the path with the River Maun on the right. In a little over

¼ mile (400 metres) follow the path round to the right keeping close to the flood dyke and edge of the field; the River Maun is just beyond this.

10 Turn right and cross two bridges, one over the flood dyke and the other over the River Maun, and follow the path round to the left keeping the river on the left. Follow this for ⅓ mile (530 metres) to the road on the outskirts of the village of Edwinstowe.

11 Continue ahead on the road, past houses, to the Rufford Road (B6034) and the roadsign 'Major Oak'.

12 Turn left and walk through Edwinstowe **E**, passing the end of Robin Hood's Way **D**, through the shopping area, to the road junction with the A6075 which is beside the Royal Oak inn.

13 Cross the road and keep straight ahead on Church Street, passing St Mary's Church **F** on the left. Continue for 200 yards (180 metres) to the perimeter of Sherwood Forest Country Park. Leave the road and follow the path on the left, past the cricket field and back into the Visitors' Centre car park.

the summer the ground is covered with bracken but earlier in the year spring flowers such as bluebells, primroses and wood anemones are a common sight.

This mixed woodland is host to a wide variety of birds, such as blackbirds, thrushes, redpolls, robins, starlings, cuckoos in summer, tree creepers, woodpeckers and the colourful jay. Grey squirrels are seen frequently and there are a few red and fallow deer in the forest, though these are rarely spotted.

Archway Lodge **C** was originally built in 1842 by the fourth Duke of Portland — who resided

▲ The neo-Gothic flamboyance of the 19th-century Archway Lodge and its setting in the fabled forest make it look rather like a fairytale castle. The niches in its walls are adorned by statues of the legendary Robin Hood and five of his companions.

◄ The River Maun flows peacefully through the landscape.

nearby at Welbeck Abbey — as a hunting lodge. It is a replica of Worksop Priory gatehouse and built in a flamboyant neo-Gothic style. In the wall niches stand local figures — in the south wall Robin Hood, Little John and Maid Marian, and the north wall has King Richard, Friar Tuck and Alan-a-Dale. It is now a private house and not, unfortunately, open to the public.

Passing through Edwinstowe and Sherwood Forest are two long distance walks. The Robin Hood's Way **D**, which has a bow and arrow blaze to mark its course, is 88 miles (140 km) long. The walk begins at Nottingham Castle and ends at Edwinstowe. The Little John Challenge Walk is a 28 mile (48 km) circular challenge walk starting from and finishing at Edwinstowe. Those who complete the circuit within 12 hours receive an embroidered badge and certificate.

THE HOLY PLACE OF EDWIN

Edwinstowe **E** is named after Edwin, King of Northumbria. It is said he fought a battle nearby against King Penda of Mercia in AD 633. Edwin was killed in the battle and his supporters carried his body to a clearing in the forest and buried him. A little later a small chapel was built. Edwin was a Christian, and to this day a cross and plaque mark the spot of St Edwin's Chapel. The place became known as Edwinstowe — the holy place of Edwin.

The parish church **F**, dedicated to St Mary, is mentioned in the Domesday Book but the oldest surviving part dates from Norman times. The 32-foot (9 metre) high Norman tower has 3 foot (1 metre) thick walls and the 'broach' spire above was built about 1450. St Mary's contains many interesting features and it is closely linked with the traditions of the forest.

▼ *The parish church of St Mary's is beautiful inside and out. Apart from its claim to have been the church where Robin and Maid Marian were married, it has other links with the forest. After a storm in 1680 the villagers were granted permission from the king to cut enough oak from the forest to pay for the repairs to the church.*

MARY EVANS PICTURE LIBRARY

The Legend of Robin Hood

The legend of Robin Hood, his Merry Men and Maid Marian is one of the most romantic and well-known stories in English folklore. There are so many varying accounts of the tale that it is impossible to get to the truth of it.

Some versions have Robin as a nobleman, the dispossessed Earl of Huntingdon, and others claim he lived and worked in Barnsdale Forest in Yorkshire. But in spite of the fact that there is no documentary evidence to connect anyone called Hood, clad in 'Lincoln Green', with a band of outlaws in Sherwood Forest, hunting the King's deer, robbing the rich and giving to the poor, and leading the Sheriff of Nottingham a merry dance, this is the most popular view of the famous 12th-century folk hero.

Another explanation for the Robin Hood legend is that it could have its roots in ancient pagan beliefs. There was a Teutonic wood spirit called Hudekin (Hood), so Robin of the Wood could be connected with this mythological creature.

So popular is the legend that all over the Midlands there are Robin Hood Inns, Little John wells and places where Robin Hood and Maid Marian were married.

One such place is under the yew tree in Doveridge, close to the Derbyshire/Staffordshire boundary. Friar Tuck is said to have held services at Lud Church, a narrow cleft in the gritstone rock near The Roaches in Staffordshire. Little John, Robin Hood's faithful companion, lies buried in Hathersage churchyard in the Peak District. And Robin Hood himself reputedly died at Kirklees Priory, near Liversedge, in West Yorkshire.

ALONG THE RIVER TRENT

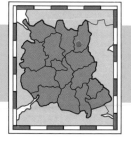

A riverbank walk through a valley of fertile farmland

The walk is mostly on defined level footpaths, along the banks of the River Trent to the outskirts of Caythorpe, following a segment of the Trent Valley Way. A short road walk brings you to the old mill there, which is no longer in use, and to a path across the fields to the village of Gunthorpe.

RIVER TRAFFIC

The final stages follow a lane, with a brief road walk through the village back to the starting-point. The River Trent is busy here, popular with narrowboats and pleasure cruisers, which use Gunthorpe Lock to avoid boating through Gunthorpe Weir.

The walk begins beside the River Trent, with views to the wooded

ROBERT EAMES. INSET: PAUL STERRY/NATURE PHOTOGRAPHERS LTD

▲ *Wild flowers border the River Trent, which has been a trading route for many centuries. The shoveler (inset) is seen in areas of shallow, open water that provide plentiful food.*

slopes of the Trent Hills on the eastern side of the river. The first half of the walk is along the banks of the navigable river, passing Gunthorpe Lock and having views of the impressive Gunthorpe Weir. A water-ski club operates near Gunthorpe Bridge. A variety of birds can be seen, including the grey heron. After visiting the old mill at Caythorpe, which still has its waterwheel, you return across the fields.

The bridge at Gunthorpe **Ⓐ** is the only road bridge across the river between Nottingham and Newark — a distance of 24 miles (39 km). The present bridge was built in 1927. Before 1875, when the first bridge at this location was built, a ferry operated here, running across the river to East Bridgford.

TRENT VALLEY WAY

The early section of the walk follows the Trent Valley Way **Ⓑ**. This is a long-distance footpath that runs alongside the River Trent from the northern boundary of Nottinghamshire to Nottingham. The River Trent **Ⓒ** is one of the major rivers of the Midlands, navigable from here to the Humber, an approximate distance of 11 miles (16.6 km). Including the lock at Gunthorpe, the river has 12 locks. Two Bronze Age dug-out canoes

FACT FILE

⚹ Gunthorpe, beside River Trent on the A6097, 10 miles (16 km) east of Nottingham

🖭 Pathfinder 813 (SK 64/74), grid reference SK 682437

miles 0	1	2	3	4	5	6	7	8	9	10 miles
kms 0	1 2 3 4 5	6	7 8	9 10 11	12 13	14 15 kms				

◔ Allow 1½ hours

▬ Level walking on defined paths beside the River Trent and along the edges of fields. Paths along field edges can be overgrown in summer months. All have stiles and footbridges. Walking boots advised

Ⓟ At Gunthorpe on Lock Road and at the British Waterways Board Car Park at Gunthorpe Lock. Both just off the A6097 road

🍴 Anchor Inn, Tom Brown's Bar and Unicorn Hotel at
🚾 Gunthorpe. Shop at Gunthorpe
🍺 Marina. Black Horse Inn at Caythorpe

THE WALK

GUNTHORPE – CAYTHORPE

The walk begins at the car park in Gunthorpe, beside the River Trent.

1 From car park, walk along the river bank in an easterly direction, away from Gunthorpe Bridge **Ⓐ**. At the end of the field keep to the bank, past the Toll House and Gunthorpe Marina on your left. Soon afterwards, pass the British Waterways Board offices and car park. Continue along Trent Valley Way **Ⓑ** to Gunthorpe Lock.

2 Go through the double white gates — a feature of this part of the River Trent **Ⓒ** — and walk along the bank for a little over 1 mile (1.6 km), passing the 17 km and 18 km markers. Opposite the wooded slopes of the Trent Hills can be seen.

3 Shortly after passing the 18 km marker, cross a footbridge and double gates. After 44 yards (40 metres), bear diagonally left to a wooden stile in the corner of the field. Cross this and bear right, keeping to the edge of the field until you reach the Hoveringham Road, gained by a stile beside a footpath sign.

4 Turn left and walk along Hoveringham Road for approximately ½ mile (800 metres) to Caythorpe and the Black Horse Inn on your right. Turn left at Mill House; the footpath is signposted.

5 The path keeps to the right-hand side of the drive, passing the mill, with its wheel visible through a window. Keep to the right of the garage to gain a stile. Continue a short distance with the field boundary on your right to the next stile. When you have gone over the stile and then a footbridge, keep the field hedge on your left and you will reach a footbridge and, within 100 yards (90 metres), another footbridge. Turn right here with the field boundary on your right. After approximately 200 yards (180 metres), turn sharp left on a path that may be overgrown, and in another 200 yards (180 metres) gain a track beside a footpath sign. The footpath becomes Peck Lane and leads to the main road in Gunthorpe.

6 Turn left and walk along the main street, passing the Anchor Inn, Tom Brown's Bar and Unicorn Hotel back to your starting-point.

◄The River Trent runs through a valley of mixed farmland and is still regarded by many as the dividing line between northern and southern England. The bridge at Gunthorpe (right) was built in 1927.

During the 19th century, the River Trent was a major artery in the waterways of the Midlands. Further work was completed in 1926, which dramatically increased traffic. However, as with all canals and navigable rivers, competition from the railways and, later, the roads greatly reduced the use of the river and its profitability.

were found in the river bed near Nottingham, providing proof that the River Trent was used as a trading route in 1000 BC.

HISTORY OF THE RIVER

The Romans in AD 120 built the Foss Dyke, linking the river to the River Witham at Lincoln. The Vikings ventured up the river on their raids. Some of the oldest bridges in England span the Trent; one in Nottingham stood for 714 years. In 1699 an Act of Parliament was passed to make the River Trent navigable, but it was not until an Act of 1783 that towpaths were built and the Trent Navigation Company was formed. Locks and weirs were built and sections were deepened.

NIC BROOMHEAD INSET: N.A.CALLOW/NHPA

A red-brick village where the Middle Ages live on

The manor of Laxton, through which this walk passes, maintains the medieval system of open-field strip farming that was the norm before the enclosures of the 17th, 18th and 19th centuries. The village consists of two compact streets surrounded by four large open fields. There are few outlying farms; the farmhouses occupy strips of land off the village streets.

Laxton's unique position is explained in its Visitor Centre **A**,

FACT FILE

☀ Laxton, 6 miles (9.6km) north of Newark, off the A616

🗺 Pathfinder 780 (SK 66/76), grid reference SK 723670

miles 0 1 2 3 4 5 6 7 8 9 10 miles
kms 0 1 2 3 4 5 6 7 8 9 10 11 12 13 14 15 kms

◔ Allow 3 hours

▭ Wide, grassy lanes, good tracks and roads in gently rolling country. Some arable fields, which may be muddy or ploughed up

P Car park at Laxton Visitor Centre

T Infrequent bus service from Tuxford to Laxton, Tel. (0115) 924 0000

🍺 Pubs in Laxton and Kneesall

WC Laxton Visitor Centre

I Laxton Visitor Centre

▲*North of the route lies West Field, one of Laxton's four open fields that was farmed in furlong strips. The meadow grasshopper (inset) is a common species that may be seen or heard by the path.*

where the walk begins. The Centre was opened in July 1986, and is able to cater for casual visitors and serious students alike. A map of the open fields is housed a short distance away in what used to be a pinfold, a pound for stray cattle.

MILL FIELD

There is much of interest in the village itself, but the route first explores the surrounding farmland. You leave the village heading south on the road towards Kneesall, then turn off on a wide, grassy lane across Mill Field **B**, one of Laxton's four great open fields. Mill Field and South Field each cover areas of around 600 acres (240 hectares), while the other two, East Field and West Field, are about half that size.

THE WALK

LAXTON – KNEESALL

The starting point of the walk is in the car park at Laxton Visitor Centre **Ⓐ**.

1 Turn right as you leave the car park, and then bear right along the road signposted to Kneesall for about ½ mile (800m), bearing right at a fork.

2 Just after passing a wood on your left, turn right down a wide green lane. This eventually narrows, and becomes a headland path with a hedge on the left. At the end of the hedge, continue straight on to a junction of tracks in the middle of Mill Field **Ⓑ**. Turn left, and follow this clear track across a valley for just over 1¼ miles (2km) to a metalled road.

3 Turn right. After 400 yards (360m), bear left, then left again. Just beyond Old Hall Farm **Ⓒ** on your right, bear left to reach St Bartholomew's Church **Ⓓ**.

4 Just past the church, turn left down School Lane. Where the lane turns to the right, take the signposted path straight ahead across a field and a playing field to the road. Turn right. After 220 yards (200m), turn left down the signposted lane to Laxton (this is the way you first approached Kneesall). Follow this for about ½ mile (800m).

5 Take a signposted path half-right to a waymarked gap in the hedge. Turn half-right, and head towards the farm buildings on the other side of the valley. At the bottom of the valley, go through a gap in the hedge, and turn left along the headland with the hedge on your left. At the end of the field, go through another gap to maintain your direction under a pylon to a bridge and a gate. Cross, and head diagonally right to a gap in the hedge.

Through the gap, bear right to a gate onto a road. Turn left along the road for just over ½ mile (800m).

6 At the end of the wood on your right, a track leads off left; take the path diagonally left

between the two towards Laxton's church **Ⓔ**. Cross a footbridge and head uphill, passing to the left of the church. Turn left onto the road, then right up a gated track through a farmyard for 350 yards (320m). When the track bends left, go right past the motte and bailey of the castle **Ⓕ** for about 80 yards (70m), then right again across the fields back to the road.

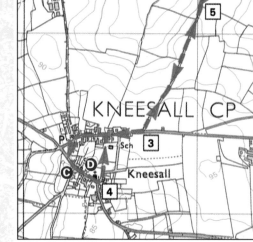

◄The Visitor Centre in Laxton contains much information about the history of open-field strip farming in the village. The Midlands are particularly rich in examples of this farming system but Laxton remains the best preserved.

The route continues through gently rolling arable farmland. You walk along wide, grassy tracks, used for centuries to gain access to the narrow strips of land in the open fields, to the village of Kneesall.

Like Laxton, this is a farming village built mostly of red brick and, in Old Hall Farm **Ⓒ**, possesses one of the oldest brick houses in the county. It was built in the early16th century as a hunting lodge by Sir John, 1st Lord Hussey, the chief butler of England. Although it has been much altered since, its mellow

MIKE WILLIAMS

ALL PHOTOS : MIKE WILLIAMS

▲*In the early 1500s, when Sir John Hussey built Old Hall Farm (above), the sunken green lane (below) that crosses Mill Field would have been regularly used by farmers and their livestock.*

red-brick and terracotta details still command attention.

A little way up the road is the parish church ❶, dedicated to St Bartholomew. Its tall tower, dating from 1425, is a local landmark, and features angels where most would have gargoyles. Inside, there are fragments of an Anglo-Saxon cross, and some old wooden bench-ends.

ALONG THE HEDGEROWS

You return to Laxton through a more familiar rural landscape of small fields separated by hedgerows, a system that seems timelessly and quintessentially English, though it is almost entirely the creation of the last 250 years.

Just outside Laxton, you leave the road to take a footpath across to the Church of St Michael ❶, whose best feature is its clerestory, built at the end of the 15th century by Archbishop Rotherham to mark his short tenure as lord of the manor.

HISTORICAL MONUMENTS

Inside, there are monuments from the 13th and 14th centuries, dedicated to previous lords of the manor, the de Everingham family. In the north aisle is a lovely screen dating from 1532, the gift of Robert Trafford, Vicar of Laxton.

Opposite the church, a lane leads to the remains of Laxton Castle ❶, which include the largest and best preserved motte and bailey in the

county. The motte stands 71 feet (21m) high, and has a circumference of 816 feet (248m). It is still possible to see the remains of a dry moat and some of the ground plan.

LAXTON CASTLE

Little is known of the history of the castle, though it is thought to have been built by the Norman John de Caux, empowered to build a castle here by William I. It was probably at its best in the 13th century. In 1205, it was visited by King John, while in 1290, Queen Eleanor,

▼*The Church of St Bartholomew in the village of Kneesall has a plain stone tower which was erected in 1425.*

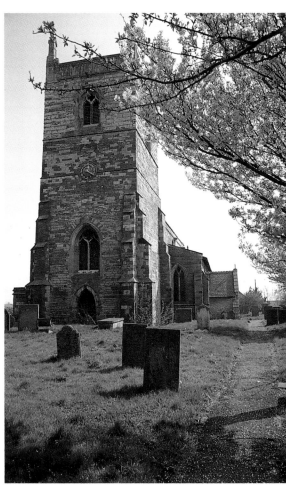

wife of Edward I, stayed here as a guest of the de Everingham family on her way from Rufford to Lincoln. It fell into disuse when the de Everingham line died out towards the end of the 14th century.

From the castle, it is a short walk back to the village, where the Dovecote Inn is worth a visit. It is here, towards the end of each year,

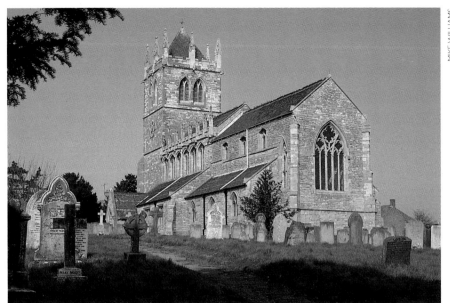

that the manor's Court Leet meets, with much of its procedure based on medieval precedent. The Court appoints a jury to inspect the fields and ensure that farmers are not encroaching, calls the manorial roll, appoints officials, agrees fines and discusses general business. At other times of the year, the Inn is simply a good place to relax after your walk.

▲*Laxton's impressive Church of St Michael, which contains monuments to the de Everingham family.*

▶*A view from the earthworks of Laxton Castle, Nottinghamshire's largest motte and bailey.*

Strip Farming

Some authorities trace the origins of strip farming to the Saxons, but it did not become widespread until the 12th and 13th centuries. The open fields in each manor were divided into narrow strips, usually 220 yards (200m) long, and these were allocated to the farmers of the village each year. In this way, everyone theoretically got equal use of the good land and the bad.

Each farmer ploughed up and down the strips, throwing the earth towards the centre to make a ridge, while each strip was separated from its neighbour by a double furrow. The characteristic pattern this created led to the system becoming known as 'ridge and furrow' farming.

The enclosure of the large, common fields by hedges began piecemeal in the 15th and 16th centuries. By the time enclosure became government policy, with the appointment of Parliamentary Commissioners in the middle of the 18th century, the old methods had dwindled except in the Midlands, where they were still widespread.

A map of the 'Manor and Lordship of Laxton', showing its cultivation in 1635. The green area at top left is Westwood Common and east of it is West Field.

These processes did not wholly pass Laxton by. From 1642, a succession of owners of the main manor enclosed several meadows and fields, and consolidated the ownership of many outer strips, some of which were as much as 3 miles (4.8km) from the centre of the village.

At the start of this period, 1,894 acres (758 hectares) were divided into 2,280 strips, while today there are 483 acres (193 hectares) in 164 strips. The manor was sold to the Ministry of Agriculture in 1952, and they reduced the number of farms working the strips to 14.

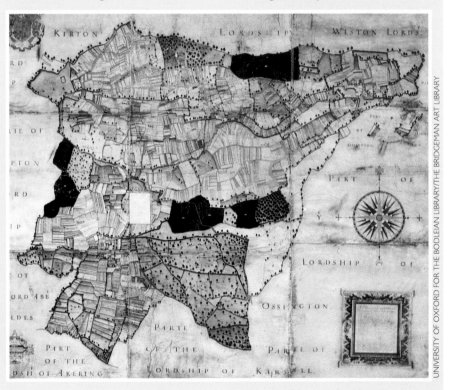

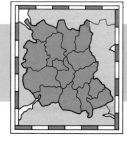
NOTTINGHAMSHIRE

Along the Chesterfield Canal from an attractive hilltop village

Gringley on the Hill has a remarkable position, spread along a ridge at the end of a long range of low hills that stretches from Nottingham. The village is attractive by any standards, with many fine houses on its steep hills. The walk begins just east of Beacon Hill **Ⓐ**, a green mound at the very end of the ridge. Opinions differ as to whether it is natural or artificial; some say it was built by the Romans and others that it contains a Viking burial place.

From the top, there is a panorama stretching for 20 to 30 miles (32 to 48km). Lincoln Cathedral is visible to the east on a clear day, while to

FACT FILE

✳ Gringley on the Hill, 7 miles (11.2km) east of Bawtry, on the A631

◰ Pathfinders 728 (SK 69/79) and 745 (SK 68/78), grid reference SK 744906

miles 0	1	2	3	4	5	6	7	8	9	10 miles
kms 0	1 2 3 4 5	6 7 8 9 10 11 12 13 14 15 kms								

◓ Allow at least 3 hours

▬ Mostly good paths and tracks. One steep ascent on a road. Some field paths likely to be muddy in winter

🅿 Lay-by off the A631 at the eastern end of the village

🆃 Various buses to Gringley on the Hill and Clayworth, Tel. (0115) 924 0000 for details

🛏🍴 The Blue Bell pub and the Cross Keys pub in Gringley on the Hill, the Brewers Arms pub and the Blacksmith's Arms pub in Clayworth, and the Griff Inn in Drakeholes all serve food. Restaurant at Royston Manor Hotel, Clayworth

▲Built over 200 years ago, the Chesterfield Canal winds gently across the countryside. It closed to commercial traffic in 1955. Common skullcap (inset) is found near the water. The Butter Cross (below) at Gringley on the Hill is little more than a column today.

ROBERT EAMES

the north stretch some of the flattest, least-populated and quietest acres of England: the Isle of Axholme, the carrs, Hatfield Moors and Hatfield Chase. No land north of here, until the Yorkshire Wolds, rises more than 30 feet (9m). The hill has been used for beacon fires, and in the 1920s and 30s it was a popular spot for radio enthusiasts. Every Rogation Monday, a procession climbs to the top to ask for God's blessing.

◄ *At Clayworth there is the brick tower of a windmill. Built in 1830, it has lost its wooden cap and sails.*

The annual procession begins at the Church of St Peter and St Paul **B**, a mainly Perpendicular building with a Norman door in the base of the tower, and a classical 17th-century door in the north aisle. The church's beautiful shaft piscina, a basin and drain for washing holy vessels, is over 600 years old.

BUTTER CROSS

The Butter Cross **C** is set at the junction of Cross Hill and the High Street, just beyond the church, though nobody knows how long it has been there. Only the upright

THE WALK

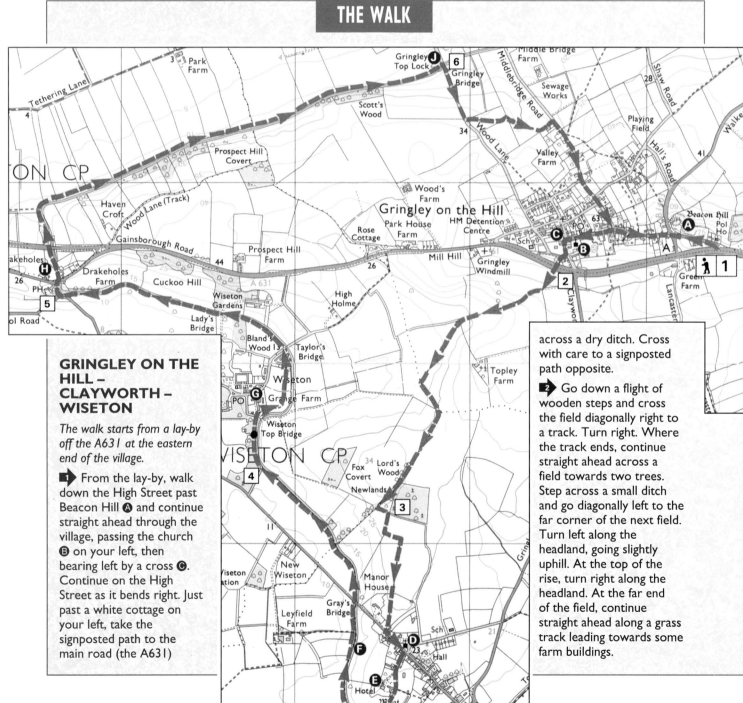

GRINGLEY ON THE HILL – CLAYWORTH – WISETON

The walk starts from a lay-by off the A631 at the eastern end of the village.

1 From the lay-by, walk down the High Street past Beacon Hill **A** and continue straight ahead through the village, passing the church **B** on your left, then bearing left by a cross **C**. Continue on the High Street as it bends right. Just past a white cottage on your left, take the signposted path to the main road (the A631)

across a dry ditch. Cross with care to a signposted path opposite.

2 Go down a flight of wooden steps and cross the field diagonally right to a track. Turn right. Where the track ends, continue straight ahead across a field towards two trees. Step across a small ditch and go diagonally left to the far corner of the next field. Turn left along the headland, going slightly uphill. At the top of the rise, turn right along the headland. At the far end of the field, continue straight ahead along a grass track leading towards some farm buildings.

now remains. On market days the farmers' wives sat on its steps selling their eggs and butter.

The route heads across fields, passing a 4-storey windmill that dates from 1830, to Clayworth. The village straddles the old Roman road between Doncaster and Lincoln. Most of the houses on the narrow main street date from the 1700s. Clayworth was once famous for its

Nature Walk

RICHARD BONSON

A voracious hunter, found in all but fast-flowing rivers, THE PIKE has backward-pointing teeth, which prevent prey from escaping. It lays its eggs on water plants.

◀*Crossing the canal at Wiseton, this attractive bridge carries the drive to Wiseton Hall. The recently restored Griff Inn (below) was designed to enhance the view from the Hall.*

BOTH PHOTOS: ROBERT EAMES

celery — the Clayworth Pink variety originated here — and the common land was divided between the villagers for growing this crop.

St Peter's Church **D** has a base that dates from before the Norman Conquest, but the building is Perpendicular. There is a rare, 14th-century stone screen inside, and much Victorian decoration and stained glass, as well as memorials to the families of Royston Manor **E**, which is now a hotel. The Manor's south front is said to date from 1588, but everything visible from the road was rebuilt in 1891. This was the ancestral home of the Otter family until they sold their lands in 1948.

UNSPOILT VILLAGE

Otter's Bridge leads you onto the Chesterfield Canal **F** (see box). The canal takes you past Wiseton **G**, a completely unspoilt village of cottages dating from the 18th and 19th

3 Pass the farm buildings on your left, and bear left on the track. At the first hedge, turn right, and walk across an arable field to its far corner. Climb the stile and walk between a wire fence and a hedge. Pass through a gap in the hedge and follow a worn grass path to a signpost by a metalled road. Turn left towards the church **D**. Opposite the church, turn right down St Peters Lane to pass Royston Manor

Hotel **E** on your right. Cross the bridge over the canal **F**, and follow the towpath to the right for just over 1 mile (1.6km) to Wiseton **G**, passing under bridge No. 69.

4 Where the towpath joins a metalled road, turn right. Where the road bears away, rejoin the towpath, passing under bridge No. 70. Follow the towpath for 1¼ miles (2km) to Drakeholes **H**.

5 At a picnic site, turn onto the main road and walk uphill across the tunnel. Cross the main road with care. Take the gravel track opposite and follow it to the left of some farm buildings as it becomes a grassy track. Follow the track back down to the canalside and go ahead under a road bridge (No. 73A). Follow the towpath for nearly 1¼ miles (2km) to Gringley Top Lock **J**.

6 Pass in front of the lock-keeper's cottage and under bridge No. 74, then turn left up the steps. Turn left uphill along the road. After 350 yards (315m) take a signposted footpath on your left. Walk to the far right corner of the field. Climb the stile and go diagonally right, heading to the right of two large barns. Climb two stiles onto a road, and turn right. At the centre of Gringley, turn left to reach the start.

centuries. You pass under an ornamental bridge, over which passes the drive to Wiseton Hall. The hall was built in 1771 and demolished in 1960. Just the 18th-century stables survive. The Acklam family first owned the hall; a member of the family, Jonathan Acklam, did much to improve the estate. From 1814 to 1863 it was owned by the Spencers, ancestors of the Princess of Wales.

DRAKEHOLES TUNNEL

Drakeholes Tunnel ❽ was a natural place for a busy wharf in the canal's heyday; the boats were forced to stop to harness or unharness the

▲*Narrowboats still tie up at the once-busy wharf before the 154-yard long Drakeholes Tunnel.*

horses because of the 154-yard (138.6-m) tunnel, and the road is nearby. A regular packetboat service operated from here.

The Griff Inn, next to the tunnel, was built in the early 1800s, and until recently was known as The White Swan. The landlord was responsible for organizing the wharf and cargoes, and stage coaches called here from places such as Sheffield, Louth, Gainsborough and Lincoln. Jonathan Acklam of Wiseton Hall had a hand in the design of the hotel, because he wished to see decorative buildings from his terrace. As the canal declined, so did the trade of the pub, but it was completely restored and reopened in 1982. Opposite the pub, a pair of lodges, now rather dilapidated, mark the old entrance to Wiseton Hall.

Further along the canal is Gringley Top Lock ❿, a wide lock with a cottage, still occupied, that dates from the opening of the canal. From here, the walk returns to the village of Gringley across the fields and up a steep street into the village centre.

The Chesterfield Canal

This fine waterway was built fairly early in the 'Canal Age' at the end of the 18th century, when barges and narrowboats became the main means of transporting the raw materials and finished products of the burgeoning Industrial Revolution.

It was surveyed by the first great canal engineer, James Brindley, and completed five years after his death. The 46-mile (73.4-km) waterway, running from Chesterfield to West Stockwith on the Trent, was formally opened on 4 June 1777.

Stone, corn, lead, bricks and general goods were carried, but the

The wide basin at Drakeholes gives boats plenty of room to manoeuvre.

main cargo was coal. From West Stockwith, goods went on downriver with the tide or under sail.

The way the canal winds through the contours of the land rather than cutting across them gives a clue as to its early date. Extensive embankments and cuttings were beyond the scope of the canal pioneers. The one and only great feat of engineering on the canal was the 2,895-yard (2,730-m) Norwood Tunnel.

Like all other canals, the Chesterfield suffered in the 19th century from the competition of the railways. Trade declined, and after 1888 it ran at a loss. The Norwood Tunnel, whose roof had collapsed several times over the years, was closed in 1908, cutting off a long section of canal.

After 1955, the waterway stopped being used commercially and fell into almost total ruin, though the towpath continued in use as a bridleway, and remained in good condition. In 1961, a group of enthusiasts teamed up to save the 26 navigable miles (41.6km) remaining. The Chesterfield Canal Society now represents all parties with an interest in the canal, and is currently working on the remaining 20 miles (32km). The Society even has high hopes of repairing the Norwood Tunnel, restoring the canal to full working order.

▼*To the north of Gringley on the Hill is Gringley Top Lock, which has been restored to full working order.*

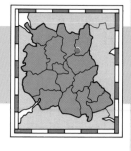

LAWRENCE COUNTRY

◄*D H Lawrence was born in this unassuming terraced cottage in Eastwood on 11 September 1885. Wood blewit (inset) adorns High Park Wood.*

SUE MORRIS. INSET: C.H. GAMERSALL/NATURE PHOTOGRAPHERS

FACT FILE

⚹ Eastwood, 7½ miles (12km) north-east of Nottingham, just off the A610

OS Pathfinders 812 (SK 44/54) and 795 (SK 45/55), grid reference SK 465470

miles 0 1 2 3 4 5 6 7 8 9 10 miles
kms 0 1 2 3 4 5 6 7 8 9 10 11 12 13 14 15 kms

◑ Allow 4 hours plus time to visit the museum and library

▬ Field footpaths and pavements; some moderately steep ascents and descents

P Car park at Lawrence Birthplace Museum

T Regular buses from Victoria Bus Station, Nottingham

▦ Several pubs in Eastwood

🍴 Tea-rooms opposite Museum

WC Next to Eastwood Library

⌂ Lawrence Museum open daily, Apr-Oct 10am-5pm, Nov-Mar 10am-4pm. Eastwood Library open Mon, Tue, Thu, 9.30am-7pm; Fri 9.30am-6pm, Sat 9.30am-1pm; closed Wed, Sun. Other Lawrence houses in Eastwood not open to the public.

An exploration of the countryside that inspired a famous writer

Four years before his death, the author D H Lawrence wrote of the view from his former home in Eastwood: 'I know that view better than any in the world...that's the country of my heart'. The memory of this landscape remained a powerful influence on him and his writing.

The character of the Eastwood area has changed since Lawrence's day, around the turn of the century.

The grimy collieries and pit-head winding wheels are gone. Tractors ply the steep sides of the once-black spoil heaps, mowing hay, and the rows of miners' cottages have been attractively refurbished. However, many of the places Lawrence wrote about have changed very little.

Eastwood, the 'Bestwood' of *Sons and Lovers*, is a bustling little town. Close behind the busy shops of Nottingham Road is Victoria Street; the walk begins here at number 8A, the Lawrence Birthplace Museum **A**,

▶*The young Lawrence attended the red-brick, Victorian Beauvale Board School.*

SUE MORRIS

THE WALK

EASTWOOD – GREASLEY – MOORGREEN RESERVOIR

The walk starts at the Lawrence Birthplace Museum **A**, *Victoria Street, Eastwood.*

1 Go south on Victoria Street to Nottingham Road. Turn left. Continue past the library **B** and go left down Walker Street. Pass number 8 **C** and continue to the junction with Lynncroft Road.

2 Turn right and continue past number 97 **D** to Dovecote Road. Turn left and walk to the junction of Mill Lane and Beauvale, past the (Greasley) Beauvale Board School **E**. Continue past the Ram Inn and Poplar Farm on the left. Take the footpath right signposted 'Watnall and Kimberley'.

3 Cross two fields, then turn left to Greasley's church **F**. Climb the stile, cross the churchyard and turn right on the road to the entrance of Greasley Castle Farm **G**.

4 Cross and take the footpath opposite by the Lawrence information sign. Follow the path uphill, then

down around a wide bend to the right, and a right-angled bend to the left at the bottom of the hill. Continue straight ahead across the field. Follow the path as it bends right to Brooksbreasting Farm. At the farm, take the lane left.

Continue past the edge of the wood and a signpost for 'Hucknall, Annesley, Underwood'. Go as far as the bend for a sight of the remains of Beauvale Priory **H**. Return to the signpost.

5 Turn left to the motorway. Go left across

a field and enter the wood via a waymarked stile. Follow the public footpath ahead. Turn right on a major shale-surfaced crossing path and follow it uphill to reach the edge of the wood.

6 Cross two waymarked

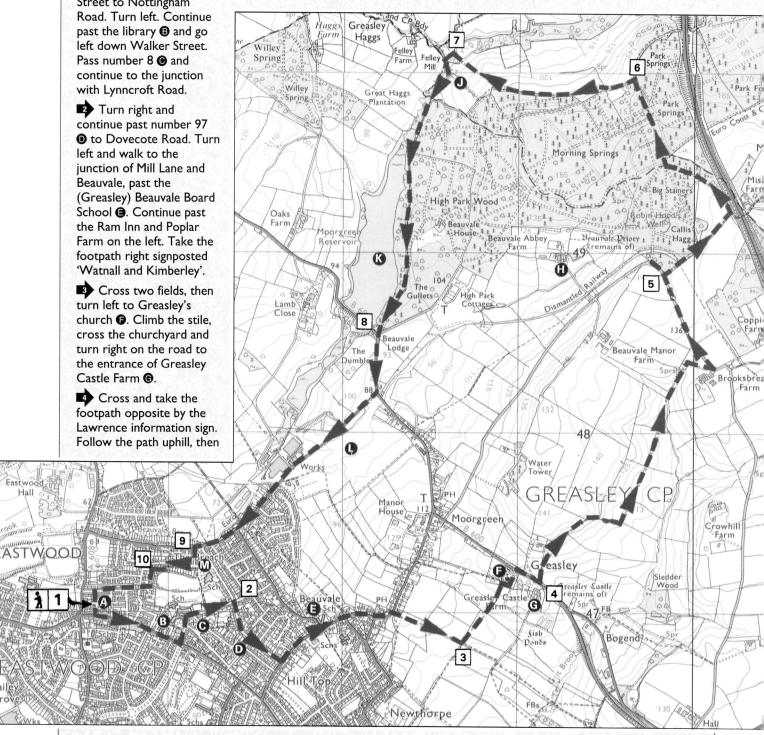

stiles, and follow the path as it swings left. Follow the cart-track, the wood on your left, to the bottom of the valley. Ignore the waymarked minor path forking left alongside the wood, ¾ of the way down.

7 Turn left off the cart-track onto a concrete lane. The ruins of Felley Mill **J** are soon visible on the left.

Leave the lane through a gap on the left, which drops down to a stream. Do not cross it; continue left, with the stream on your right, on a waymarked bridlepath through woods towards Moorgreen. Moorgreen Reservoir **K** appears on your right through the trees. Where the bridlepath joins a

tarmac drive, bear right along it to Beauvale Lodge.

8 Turn left on the road, then right at the entrance to Moorgreen Industrial Park. Follow the road past derelict Moorgreen Colliery **L**, and straight on into Eastwood.

9 Take the first left turn after Lynncroft Road. Turn right along Garden Road

— number 28 **M** is on the left — and left down the alleyway opposite Greenhills Avenue, to Atherfield Gardens.

10 Turn left. Near the top, follow the alleyway right, between the gardens. Cross Wood Street, Wellington Street and Albert Street. Go left up Victoria Street to the start.

▲*The route leads through fields with a good view of the 15th-century tower of St Mary's Church in Greasley. Haggs Farm (right), beyond High Park Wood, was a place Lawrence loved to visit.*

where the author was born in 1885.

The house has been carefully restored to reflect the lifestyle of the Victorian working class, and Lawrence's own early childhood. Displays in the adjoining building provide a good introduction to the places Lawrence knew and wrote about and the life of a coal-miner in the 1880s. Lawrence's father, Arthur, worked at nearby Brinsley Colliery from the age of seven.

◄*The tranquil waters of Moorgreen Reservoir are enjoyed by waterbirds.*

Along Nottingham Road is a modern public library **B**. A local studies room houses an extensive collection of books by and about Lawrence, including the first editions which belonged to his friend William Hopkin. On display are various letters and Lawrence's desk.

The route next passes 8 Walker Street **C**, where the Lawrence family lived from 1891-1902. From here they moved to 97 Lynncroft Road **D**, where Lawrence's beloved mother, Lydia, died in 1910.

SCHOLARSHIP

Young David attended the Beauvale Board School **E** (now the Greasley Beauvale Infants School) from 1892 to 1898. He was the first pupil from the school to win a scholarship to Nottingham High School.

On your way out of Eastwood, you pass the 'Ram Inn' of his first novel *The White Peacock* — though the Ram Inn of Lawrence's day was at 46A and B, in the building

opposite the present pub.

The fields around Greasley were where *Love among the Haystacks* was played out, and still make an attractive setting for Greasley's church **F**. St Mary's has a 15th-century tower, though much of today's building dates from the 19th century.

Inside are two medieval glass roundels, depicting St Lucy and St Agatha, that were rescued from ruined Beauvale Priory nearby. One of the most interesting graves in the churchyard is that of Benjamin Drawwater, who circumnavigated the world with Captain Cook.

Greasley was mentioned in the *Domesday Book*, and the de Cantelupes of Greasley were a prominent local family in the 13th century. Edward III gave them permission to fortify their manor, which became known as Greasley Castle and stood on the site of the present-day Greasley Castle Farm **G**.

The route continues through the fields towards High Park Wood, and the ruins of Carthusian Beauvale Priory **H**, founded by Nicholas de Cantelupe in 1343. It flourished until

1535, when the priors, John Houghton and Robert Lawrence, were executed at Tyburn for their refusal to renounce the Pope in favour of Henry VIII. All that remains now of the priory are fragments of the walls and a window among the buildings of Beauvale Abbey Farm. To view the ruins at close quarters, you must ask permission at the farm.

On the other side of the wood, there are good views of Haggs Farm, a collection of low, red buildings which nestle into the hillside up to Underwood. This was the home of the Chambers family, and Lawrence frequently visited there between 1901-1908. His relationship with young Jessie Chambers was a

Moorgreen Colliery was the 'Minton' colliery of Lawrence's Sons and Lovers. *The quadrangles of terraced miners' cottages (below) became 'The Squares'.*

great influence on his early life and writing; the character of Miriam Leivers in *Sons and Lovers* was based on her. In the novel, Haggs Farm became 'Willey Farm'.

The path descends to Felley Mill **J**, the 'Strelley Mill' of *The White Peacock*. Only the foundations of some outbuildings are still visible,

D H Lawrence (1885-1930)

A portrait of Lawrence taken in 1908, the year he finished his teacher training at University College, Nottingham.

One of a family of five, David Herbert Lawrence was a sickly child. His mother was determined to keep him out of the mines, and encouraged him at school. After winning a scholarship, he attended Nottingham High School for three years, but poverty forced him to give up his education and take a clerical job when he was 15. He eventually gained a teacher's certificate at Nottingham University College.

By this time he had started writing; his first book, *The White Peacock*, appeared in 1911, followed two years later by his first major novel, *Sons and Lovers*, which drew on his early years in the Eastwood

area. Between the two, he met Frieda Weekley, the German wife of his professor at Nottingham; they fell in love and ran off together to Germany. Lawrence was to spend the rest of his life moving around the world. His travels took him to Ceylon, Australia, America, Mexico, Italy and finally to Vence, in the south of France, where he died of tuberculosis in 1930.

Despite his wanderings, he never forgot the landscape of his youth, and other works, notably *The Rainbow* (1915), were set there. He described its appeal in 1929. 'It is hilly country, looking west to Crich and towards Matlock, sixteen miles away, and east and north-east towards Mansfield and the Sherwood Forest district. To me it seemed, and still seems, an extremely beautiful countryside, just between the red sandstone and the oak-trees of Nottingham, and the cold limestone, the ash-trees, the stone fences of Derbyshire. To me, as a child and a young man, it was still the old England of the forest and agricultural past; there were no motor cars, the mines were, in a sense, an accident in the landscape, and Robin Hood and his merry men were not very far away.'

and the millpond is overgrown, but it is still a pretty spot.

Moorgreen Reservoir **K** was built to supply the local canal network, and appears in several novels; as 'Nethermere' in *The White Peacock* and *Sons and Lovers*, and 'Willey Water' in *Women in Love*. Lawrence based the drowning incident in *Women in Love* on a real-life tragedy here. A bridleway goes through the wood alongside the reservoir.

COAL IN THE CORN

You return to Eastwood through Moorgreen Industrial Park, the site of Moorgreen Colliery **L**, closed in 1985. The pit-head buildings have been demolished, and the winding-wheel stands as a memorial at the entrance by the Moorgreen road. This was 'Minton' colliery in *Sons and Lovers*, where it was described as 'a large mine among cornfields'.

Back in Eastwood, you pass 28 Garden Road **M**, where the Lawrences lived from 1887-1891, in a part of Eastwood known as 'The Breach'. The Morel family home in *Sons and Lovers* was based on this house, and the area re-named 'The Bottoms'.

Quadrangles of terraced miners' cottages ('The Squares' in *Sons and Lovers*) line the last part of the walk. Their size gives an idea of the life of the Victorian miners, but the houses have been modernized, and their dim alleys paved and set with trees.

FACT FILE

- Thor's Cave and the Manifold Valley, north-west of Ashbourne

- Outdoor Leisure Map 24, grid reference SK 084544

miles 0 1 2 3 4 5 6 7 8 9 10 miles
kms 0 1 2 3 4 5 6 7 8 9 10 11 12 13 14 15 kms

- Allow 4 hours

- A moderately strenuous route. Steep climb up to Thor's Cave. Long slow hill climb back up to Grindon. Bridle tracks can get muddy in wet weather. Boots recommended. Not suitable for very young children, elderly or unfit people

- P Small car park and picnic site at Grindon on the north side of the church

A strenuous walk through Staffordshire's classic limestone scenery

A walk of much geological interest on the edge of the Staffordshire moorlands and the White Peak of Derbyshire. The route passes through the two attractive hill villages of Grindon and Wetton, follows the deep limestone gorge of the Manifold Valley, with its disappearing river, and climbs up to the spectacularly sited Thor's Cave, an imposing cavern which can be safely entered and explored.

The walk begins in the pretty hill village of Grindon **A**, which lies high on the 1,000-foot (304-metre) contour line. It contains many charming, old limestone buildings. The large 19th-century church, with its dominant spire, is sometimes known as the 'Cathedral of the Moor'. The interior of the church contains a Calvary tapestry with a plaque recording a tragedy in the severe winter of 1947. The village was cut off for many days because of the heavy snowfalls and food supplies began to run low. A Halifax plane was used to drop essential supplies, but crashed on Grindon

▲ *Thor's Cave is set in a limestone cliff perched high above the woodland of the Manifold Valley. Among the diverse flora of the Peak District are wild raspberries (inset), found under trees.*

Moor, killing its six RAF crew members and several bystanders.

After reaching the open country alongside the stream you come to Wetton Mill **B**. There was a corn mill here in the 19th century, but the main building now is a very pleasant café and shop. There is an interesting limestone crag to the left

THE WALK

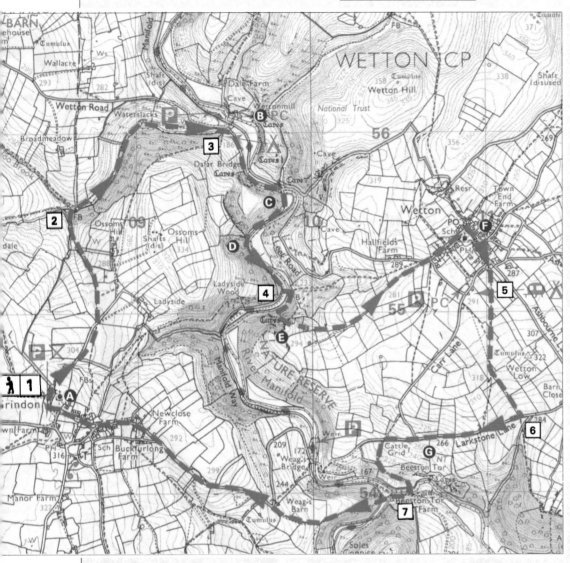

footbridge at Hoo Brook.

2 Cross the footbridge and follow the path along the side of the stream down to Wetton Mill **B**. There are toilets and a café at the mill.

3 At the intersection of tracks near Wetton Mill you will see a ford. Turn right across ford and follow the lane over Dafar Bridge, to reach a wide footbridge. Turn right over the footbridge and follow the tarmac track, that is the old railway line **C**. At the bend in the river, there is a fine view of Thor's Cave ahead. The river normally begins to sink underground at this point **D**. Eventually you reach the footbridge below Thor's Cave.

4 Cross the footbridge and ascend the right-hand path that climbs steeply up to Thor's Cave **E**. This section can be slippery and muddy in wet weather. After you have explored the cave, do not return down the steps, but take the small path on your right as you leave the cave, that leads up to a way-marked stile. Follow the clearly-defined path around the edge of the field, keeping near to the boundary wall. Do not go through gap in wall leading

GRINDON – WETTON – BEESTON TOR

The walk starts at the car park by the church in Grindon **A**.

1 From car park by church in Grindon, follow the lane over cattle grid and down for about ¼ mile (400 metres) to the stile and bridleway on your left. Follow the bridleway that runs diagonally across the first field and then down through three small fields to reach the

with many small caves and fissures.

Crossing the footbridge you walk along the old railway line **C**. This track, which goes right up the valley to Hulme End and comes up the River Hamps valley from Waterhouses, was originally the Leek and Manifold Light Railway — a narrow gauge line built between 1902 and 1904 to serve the farms, quarries and mines along the dale. Although it was a delightful rural line, it never really paid its way, and eventually closed in 1934.

It was worked by two narrow gauge locomotives, which very sadly were broken up. The whole length of the line has now been turned into an attractive footpath, which is especially suitable for families, young children and elderly walkers.

Shortly you reach the part of the river known as the 'disappearing river' **D**. Except in extremely wet

▶ *One of the glorious views on the way to Wetton; visible in the distance are Thor's Cave and Grindon Church spire.*

to a barn, but stay in this field. Cross tumbledown wall into next field and head for cattle trough, with stile in wall and gateway beyond which leads onto a farm track. Bear left and follow the track that leads into Wetton ❻. At end of track, turn right onto tarmac road to Wetton village, continue right through the village staying on the tarmac road, past the church and pub, down to the road junction where side road is signposted for 'Grindon, Manifold Valley and toilets'. Turn right onto this side road, then immediately left onto track leading onto camping and caravan site.

❺ Follow the track onto the site, and look for the stile in the wall about 55 yards (50 metres) on the right. Cross the next three fields in a diagonal direction aiming for the stiles in the walls. In the fourth field, head up towards the large stone barn on the horizon. You can only see its roof from here, plus a tree on either side. Look for the stile in the wall on the left just before you reach the barn. Cross over and follow the right-hand wall down to the lane.

❻ Turn right and follow the lane for nearly ½ mile (800 metres) to the

footpath on the left by the cattle grid. Follow the clearly defined, broad green path alongside tumbledown wall. When you reach the bottom of the hill, you will have a clear view of Beeston Tor ❼ on your left. Bear right to cross over the normally dry river bed. On reaching the other bank, turn right along the track and cross the bridge. (Note: In very wet conditions, this crossing point can be under water, in which case retrace your steps uphill to the lane, turn left and descend the lane to cross the river at Weag's Bridge, turn left and follow the track to reach Stage 7.)

❼ From the bridge, bear immediately left to follow the bridleway. Cross over the old railway track, and follow the bridleway up the hill. There are various tracks up here through the thorn bushes, but generally aim upwards and to the left, keeping near to the line of telegraph poles. Once on top of the hill, keep near to telegraph poles until you see a bridlegate in the wall. Follow the bridleway up to the lane, to the left of the ruined stone barn. Continue straight on and follow the lane back to Grindon and the car park by the church.

◀ *The village of Wetton, mid-way through the route, is a narrow settlement perched high above the Manifold Valley.*

▶ *Wetton Church and the fossil-covered tomb of Samuel Carrington who carried out local archaeological excavations, including the one at Thor's Cave.*

explored safely although they are usually very muddy. Lower down the crag is Thor's Fissure Cave, which was excavated in the late 1920s to reveal an amazing range of

ALL PHOTOS MIKE WILLIAMS

conditions, the river begins to sink underground between the two footbridges. It disappears down fissures in the rock known as swallow holes. The river re-emerges further on downstream in boiling springs in the grounds of Ilam Hall. This has been proved by putting coloured dyes and corks in the water.

A little further on you arrive at Thor's Cave ❺. Entirely natural and formed by the water action on the limestone, the cave entrance is some 350 feet (107 metres) above the

river. The name may derive from the word Tor (a crag) but more likely it comes from Thor, the Norse God of Thunder. The cave is 30 feet (9 metres) high and 23 feet (7 metres) wide at the entrance, with a huge central pillar. It is now a popular site for rock climbers. Excavations have found arrow heads, bronze brooches and an iron adze, as well as a complete skeleton, thought to be Neolithic, carefully buried in an upright position. The inner passages of the cave can be

▲ *Near Wetton Mill, the bed of the Manifold River in summer shows why it is known as the 'disappearing river'.*

animal bones including bear, deer, wolf and even a dolphin.

Wetton ❻ is another charming hill village. In the church yard there is the fossil covered tomb of Samuel Carrington, the 19th-century school master who carried out the excavations in Thor's Cave. Many of his finds are now in Sheffield Museum. There is a small café in the village and a very pleasant pub.

ANIMAL BONES

The final stretch of the walk includes a clear view of Beeston Tor ❼, a large limestone buttress 600 feet (183 metres) long and 200 feet (61 metres) high. It is a popular rock climbing area with high grade climbs. About 140 feet (43 metres) up on the right-hand side is the Lynx Cave, so-called from the

▼ *The rolling countryside of the White Peak district with dry stone walls, typical of the area, and small fields.*

Limestone Geology

More than most parts of England, this area remains very much as nature fashioned it, and the landscape has not been drastically affected or altered by man.

The geological story is a complex one, but in simple terms it began about 280 million years ago, when the whole area of what is now the Peak District was covered by a warm, shallow sub-tropical sea. A huge mass of corals, shell fish and the remains of many other minute organisms were deposited in the sands and muds. These built up to over 1,700 feet (518 metres) in depth and were compressed over a long period of time to form what we now term as limestone rock. This is why so many superb fossils can be found in limestone. Look carefully

The view out of Thor's Cave across the Manifold Valley. The inset of fossils indicates the many specimens to be found due to the limestone geology of the area.

during the course of your walk, you are certain to find interesting fossils in many of the rocks and stones that you see en route.

Small, marine volcanoes were also active at this time and the minerals deposited from them found their way into the cracks and fissures of the limestone forming the lead and copper veins that have been mined for centuries in the Peak District. Then over millions of years, subterranean pressures worked to fold and uplift this limestone mass to form what geologists call the Derbyshire Dome. Streams of water from rains and snows, especially during the Ice Ages began to pour off this dome. Limestone is slightly soluble in natural water and, as the water seeped through cracks and joints in the rock, it began to dissolve away the limestone to form miles of underground stream passages and eventually great rivers and pools, thus forming complex cave systems. Many of these vast and long caverns eventually collapsed in, so forming the deep valleys and leaving exposed tributary systems such as Thor's Cave high above the present course of the river. This wearing away process of the water action continues endlessly and the Manifold Valley in particular provides all the classic features of limestone scenery with its disappearing river, swallow holes, springs and caves.

animal bones found there. Bones of reindeer and polecat were also discovered here. At the base of the tor is St Bertram's Cave, which is occasionally visited by pot-holers, although it does not extend back very far. Fifty silver Saxon coins were found in here.

The limestone cliffs and grasslands have fascinating plants. Bird cherry and globeflower sprout from crevices out of reach of grazing animals; bloody cranesbill, mountain pansy and Nottingham catchfly are among the local plants to be found here. There are also some fine butterflies. Dark green fritillaries — large, chequered orange insects — are sometimes seen over the hills, whereas a dwarf form of the orange tip can be found in the dales, where wood tiger moths also fly by day.

MIKE WILLIAMS/NATIONAL TRUST PHOTOGRAPHIC LIBRARY. INSET: DR ECKART POTT/BRUCE COLEMAN LTD

surface; a few years ago many mine sites could be seen from the high land, the loftiest point is 800 feet (244 metres) above sea level. With the decline of the industry mining has all but finished in the region.

With so much industrial despoilation around Cannock Chase it is surprising that the area retains so much unspoilt grandeur. Today many of the acres are administered by the Forestry Commission which has managed plantations of Scots and Corsican pine since the 1920s.

◄*The Tower of the Winds is one of several monuments in the parklands of Shugborough Estate. The long-eared owl (inset) is active only at night and roosts in dense foliage during the day.*

FACT FILE

- Shugborough Estate, between Rugeley and Stafford, 5 miles (8 km) east of Stafford

- Pathfinders 850 (SJ 82/92), 871 (SJ 81/91) and 851 (SK 02/12), grid reference on 851 SK 004205

miles 0 1 2 3 4 5 6 7 8 9 10 miles
kms 0 1 2 3 4 5 6 7 8 9 10 11 12 13 14 15 kms

- Allow 4 to 5 hours

- Stony and damp in places and strong, waterproof footwear is recommended

- **P** Free Forestry Commission car park is signed at Seven Springs, 3 miles (5 km) from Rugeley westwards along the A513 towards Stafford

- Inns at Little Haywood and Great Haywood

- Licensed restaurant and café alongside the canal at Great Haywood. Tearoom at Shugborough Hall

- Shugborough Hall, farm, museum and gardens. Open March-October, 11am–5pm. Admission charge. Tel. Little Haywood (01889) 881388

To an 18th-century mansion in a wide, shallow river valley

Cannock Chase, which was designated in 1958 as an 'Area of Outstanding Natural Beauty', was once a great hunting ground for kings from the days of the Saxon Kingdom of Mercia. It was a favourite place for Henry II who hunted from Radmore Lodge. However, in 1281 Edward decreed that all the wolves should be killed and the days of the Royal Forest were soon to be over; the Chase became the property of the Bishop of Lichfield. With the insatiable demand for charcoal for the iron industry until the early 19th century, much of the woodland was felled to create open heathland. Today the Chase covers some 300,000 acres (121 hectares) of wild heathlands interspersed with woodlands.

SHEEP FARMING

The region escaped much enclosure because the soil is gravelly and was considered too poor for agriculture. It did, however, support a type of grey-faced sheep peculiar to the Chase, and Cannock was once a thriving market town.

There are layers of coal under the

THE WALK

CANNOCK CHASE COUNTRY PARK – SHUGBOROUGH ESTATE

The walk begins at the car park at Seven Springs **A**.

1 From the car park walk back along the vehicle track to the A513. Cross to the lane opposite. Cross the River Trent **B** and go under the railway to the canal towing path (access on right).

2 Pass under the lane and keep by the Trent and Mersey Canal **C**, on your right side, to the next road bridge. Turn left over pack-horse bridge **D** to enter Shugborough Park. Turn right to the Hall **E**, museum and gardens. If you do not wish to visit these keep ahead. If you do visit them rejoin the park road.

3 Go by the farm museum **F** and continue along the drive. Keep a look-out for the assorted park monuments **G**. Over the decorative railway arch **H** keep ahead, so leaving the park road which turns sharp right.

4 Walk through the gates and cross a white-railed bridge over a stream. Continue to road and turn right for almost ½ mile (800 metres). Take care on this busy road, for half the distance there is no pavement.

5 Leave the road at the Punchbowl Car Park. Keep to the left-hand side of the car park to pass through a barrier and walk along a wide cinder track.

6 At a meeting of tracks turn left at the sign for Staffs Way to another junction by the stream. This is the place called

Stepping Stones **J** at the start of Sherbrook Valley.

7 Bear right along the track, keeping the brook on your left-hand side. On the other side of the valley is Dick Slee's Cave **K**.

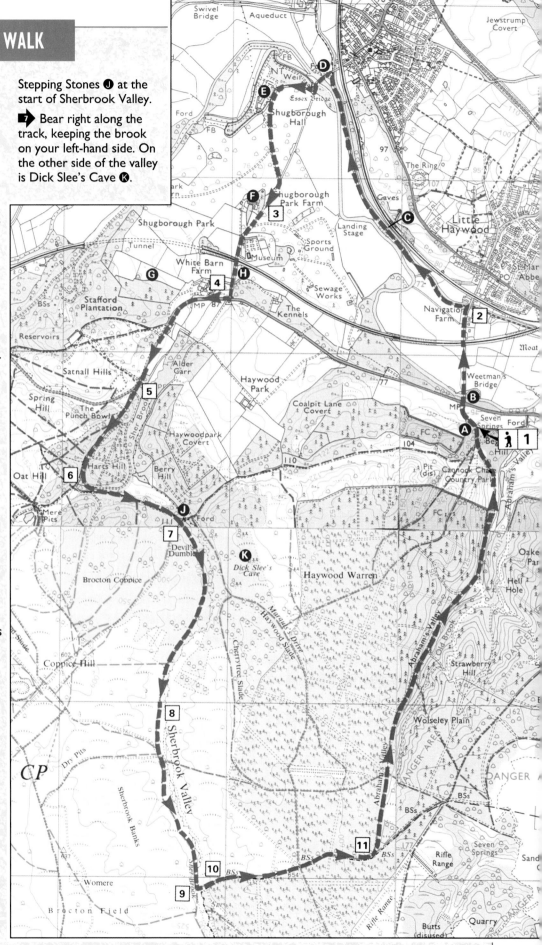

▶8 Stay on the main valley track for 1½ miles (2.4 km) ignoring many other tracks to the right and left. (There are picnic spots and tables along this track.)

▶9 Turn left to cross the brook by stepping stones and nearby pine wood to meet a joining track. Turn left so the tall pines are on your right side.

▶10 The track bears right. Ignore other side tracks and stay by the trees. At a junction by a concrete triangulation plinth keep ahead — also at a crossing forest 'road'.

▶11 Walk downhill to a junction by a white flagpole and a warning notice. Turn left along the wide track which follows a valley to the car park at Seven Springs. Bear left, ignoring any other paths to return to the start of the walk.

Near Seven Springs ❶ are small pools where herds of fallow deer come off the Chase to drink. The species came from Asia Minor and the Mediterranean area and is thought to have been brought to these shores by the Romans.

TRENT BRIDGE

Further on, the route goes over the River Trent ❷, by a cobble-stone bridge. The plaque on the bridge reads 'erected by public subscription but mainly by the liberality of Joseph Weetman in the year 1887-8'.

A straight lane leads to the Trent and Mersey Canal ❸. This canal was designed by Thomas Brindley and completed in 1777. Much of the trade in coal carried by canal came from Midland mines. Now this is a favourite place for colourful holiday craft and the waterway provides good sport for anglers and a pleasant, tranquil towpath for walkers.

After leaving the canal the River Trent is crossed again — this time over a narrow 14-arch bridge ❹, designed for pack-horses in the 17th century. (There were originally

ERIK PELHAM/NATIONAL TRUST PHOTOGRAPHIC LIBRARY

40 arches to take the route over the once marshy ground but even in its truncated state it is still the longest pack-horse bridge in England).

The attractive parkland of Shugborough is just over the river with Shugborough Hall ❺ and museum (housed in the former stables) away to the right. The gardens have interesting Victorian terraces and rose beds are a special

▲*Built in 1693, by the junction of the rivers Sow and Trent, Shugborough Hall was enlarged in the 18th century.*

feature. The drive leads past the Georgian park farm ❻ with its collection of rare animals and classical and rather bizarre monuments ❼, many erected by the English architect James 'Athenian' Stuart.

Permission was given for the main-line railway to go through the parkland in the last century, but it goes through a tunnel to minimize its intrusion. The tunnel entrances

JONATHAN PLANT

◀*Essex Bridge, which crosses the River Trent, was named after the Earls of Essex who wanted a short cut to the heights of Cannock Chase.*

▶*The Trent and Mersey Canal, during the era of commercial canal traffic, provided a cross-country route between the North and Irish Seas.*

JONATHAN PLANT

Shugborough Hall

The Hall is set in a magnificent park alongside the River Trent. It is the 18th-century ancestral home of the Earls of Lichfield. The original small house was built on the site of a palace of the Bishops of Lichfield.

The estate was originally purchased by a wealthy local lawyer William Anson in 1624. The Ansons (later to become the Earls of Lichfield) were to own Shugborough for over 300 years until it was acquired by the National Trust in 1966. Shugborough is now administered and maintained by Staffordshire County Council and houses the County Museum.

In 1720 the ownership had passed to Thomas Anson; he greatly enlarged the former house and engaged the noted Vassalli to create some magnificent decorative plaster ceilings. It was also Thomas who was responsible for the interesting features of the park.

He spent a fortune inherited from his brother (who as a voyager had captured a Spanish treasure ship) when he placed many classical temples and monuments on prominent sites. Perhaps the finest are neo-classical structures by James 'Athenian' Stuart based on drawings made in Athens including a triumphal arch copied from the Arch of Hadrian in Athens.

The County Museum recreates life in the 19th century including the original kitchens, laundry and brewhouse. A farm in the park contains rare and threatened breeds of livestock and a working flour mill.

The elegant dining room at Shugborough Hall. The colonnaded mansion houses a fine collection of 18th-century French furniture.

▲*Known as the Stepping Stones, this idyllic picnic spot is in Cannock Chase where the route joins Sherbrook Valley.*

stoats, snakes (both adders and grass snakes) and squirrels. The rare red squirrel breeds in some of the woodlands. Although most trees are softwood pines grown commercially, there are many remnants of the ancient forests including old oaks, alders and birches that favour the damper lands near the brooks.

There are vast areas of bracken and bilberries can be gathered in the autumn. The heathers are a pretty sight in the late summer months. On the marshy lands, sedges and reeds thrive in the damp conditions.

were embellished by Egyptian and medieval designs **H**.

In the Chase proper the route joins the pretty Sherbrook Valley at an idyllic spot called Stepping Stones **J** where children love to splash and chase across the water. There is a picnic site here with benches, tables and a grassed area. Alongside the brook on the hillside to the left is Dick Slee's Cave **K**. An 18th-century hermit, he lived here with only a tame hare as a companion. Some say he left home because of his debts; others because of his raucous and nagging wife.

ANCIENT PEBBLES

The track gradually climbs up the valley. The stones underfoot are round and smooth — it is estimated that the pebble beds which formed Cannock Chase were laid down some 180 million years ago.

There is a wide assortment of natural features to be seen on the walk. In the lowland valley of the River Trent and the canal, water birds such as ducks, Canada geese, coots and scurrying moorhens can be seen. Swifts and martins swoop low over the still canal waters to catch insects and the elusive kingfisher may be spotted.

In the animal kingdom the terrain suits the water voles and rats. The canal is lined with willows (which help to consolidate the banks), reeds, rushes and the purple willow herb. Fishermen hunt the coarse fish — the pike, perch and roach. A herd of deer may be spotted at dawn or dusk when it emerges to feed on grasses, leaves, shoots and berries. Visitors are asked to keep dogs well under control to avoid accidents.

Other animals on the Chase include rabbits, foxes, badgers,

▶*Cannock Chase was once the hunting ground of Kings and is now designated an Area of Outstanding Natural Beauty.*

GEOFFREY SHAKERLEY/NATIONAL TRUST PHOTOGRAPHIC LIBRARY

PHOTOS TOP & BOTTOM RIGHT JONATHAN PLANT

MILL AND KILNS

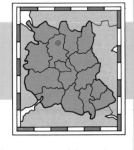

the old village lies up an old sunken lane, Hollow Lane, where this walk starts. Folds and terraces of tiny cottages and larger yeomen's houses huddle opposite a 12th-century church of mellow sandstone.

The village's former industrial centre lies below, at the foot of a

FACT FILE

- Cheddleton, 3 miles (4.8km) south of Leek, on the A520

- Pathfinders 792 (SJ 85/95), 809 (SJ 84/94) and 810 (SK 04/14), grid reference SJ 971523

  miles 0 1 2 3 4 5 6 7 8 9 10 miles
  kms 0 1 2 3 4 5 6 7 8 9 10 11 12 13 14 15 kms

- Allow 5 hours

- The route is impassable when the river floods. The river and canal section can be muddy. Several fairly short, steep ascents and descents. Walking boots are recommended

- **P** Car park between the church and the Black Lion pub, on Hollow Lane at the start

- **T** Regular bus service between Leek and Hanley stops in Cheddleton, Tel. (01785) 223344 for details

- Pubs at Cheddleton, Consallforge and Basford Bridge

▲ *An overgrown limekiln beside Caldon Canal is a reminder of the valley's industrial past, when the canal (below) was an important transport route. It has now been restored for leisure use. The cardinal beetle (left) can be seen on flowers in May and June.*

Follow a little-known river valley to a woodland nature reserve

The north-east corner of Staffordshire gloriously lays the lie that the county has been ruined by heavy industry and potteries. The River Churnet, one of the English countryside's great secrets, winds through a wooded gorge. The scenery is not disturbed by any roads. There was once industry in this valley, but it was served by canal, river, railway and tramways, all of which feature in this peaceful walk.

Cheddleton village ❶ sits astride the ancient trade route between Buxton and Stafford. The heart of

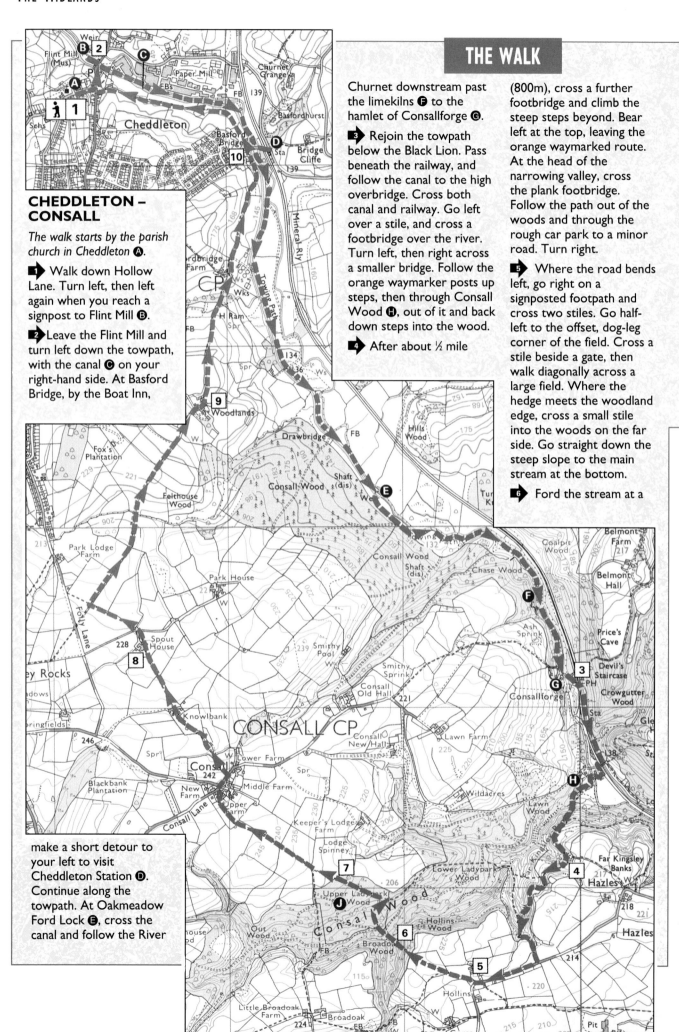

THE WALK

Churnet downstream past the limekilns **F** to the hamlet of Consallforge **G**.

3 Rejoin the towpath below the Black Lion. Pass beneath the railway, and follow the canal to the high overbridge. Cross both canal and railway. Go left over a stile, and cross a footbridge over the river. Turn left, then right across a smaller bridge. Follow the orange waymarker posts up steps, then through Consall Wood **H**, out of it and back down steps into the wood.

4 After about ½ mile

(800m), cross a further footbridge and climb the steep steps beyond. Bear left at the top, leaving the orange waymarked route. At the head of the narrowing valley, cross the plank footbridge. Follow the path out of the woods and through the rough car park to a minor road. Turn right.

5 Where the road bends left, go right on a signposted footpath and cross two stiles. Go half-left to the offset, dog-leg corner of the field. Cross a stile beside a gate, then walk diagonally across a large field. Where the hedge meets the woodland edge, cross a small stile into the woods on the far side. Go straight down the steep slope to the main stream at the bottom.

6 Ford the stream at a

CHEDDLETON – CONSALL

The walk starts by the parish church in Cheddleton **A**.

1 Walk down Hollow Lane. Turn left, then left again when you reach a signpost to Flint Mill **B**.

2 Leave the Flint Mill and turn left down the towpath, with the canal **C** on your right-hand side. At Basford Bridge, by the Boat Inn,

make a short detour to your left to visit Cheddleton Station **D**. Continue along the towpath. At Oakmeadow Ford Lock **E**, cross the canal and follow the River

sharp bend. Just beyond are a capped old shaft and a Nature Reserve sign for Upper Ladypark Wood **J**. Follow the yellow waymark arrows up to and across a wider track. The path is very indistinct. If you lose sight of the waymarks on the trees, or are in any doubt, keep right until you emerge on a wider track beside a pond filled with wiry, dead tree stumps. Go left, then bear right after a few paces along a narrow, waymarked path through the woods, again heading right if in any doubt.

7 Climb a stile out of the woods. Go slightly left to a stile in the far corner.

Follow the hedge to your right, then a field-side farm track to Upper Farm, Consall. Go through the farmyard to a road. Turn right, then left after 100 yards (90m) on the footpath signposted 'Folley Lane'. Cross the stile ahead and go up a long, thin field to Knowlbank Farm. Pass between the farmhouse and a corrugated-iron barn. Cross the farm track and head for Spout House Farm ahead.

8 Walk immediately left of a long barn. Go through the enclosed farmyard and along a drive for 50 yards (45m). At a crossing drive, go through the left-hand

gate and follow the line of the rough hedge/fence on your right to a stile. Climb this and turn right. Cross a line of stiles ahead; the path eventually merges with the walled roadway leading to the entrance to Woodlands Hall.

9 Go straight ahead through the overgrown yard into a field beyond. Stay close to a holly hedge on your left. After 100 yards (90m), cross the double stile and continue down the field with the hedge to your left. Keep ahead over another double stile. Climb the next stile and follow the farm track as it winds down through a

ford and up again between a farm and the sewage works. As the concreted road bends right, go through the middle gate ahead and follow a thorn hedge. Go through a gate, and follow the obvious path to the Boat Inn at Basford Bridge.

10 Walk in front of the terrace opposite the pub, and then along the path beyond. Take the second right fork to the canal bank, below some gardens. Remain with this path as it leaves the canal, and walk through a series of fields to return to Cheddleton at the Red Lion Inn, opposite Hollow Lane.

◀ *There are working steam locomotives and a museum at Victorian Cheddleton Station. Past Oakmeadow Ford Lock (below left) the canal joins the Churnet.*

steep sandstone bluff. Between the river and the canal are an old brewery, warehouses and the marvellous Flint Mill **B** (see box).

For nearly 4 miles (6.4km) the walk follows the Caldon Canal **C**. This was surveyed by the renowned canal-builder James Brindley, though he died before it opened in 1777. It was constructed to convey limestone from the massive quarries at Cauldon to the main Trent and Mersey Canal in Stoke-on-Trent.

RESTORED CANAL

Other uses were soon found for it, associated with the pottery industry, and it was extended to Uttoxeter in 1811. A victim of road and rail competition, it was abandoned in 1944, but in 1974 became the first canal to be fully rescued and restored by enthusiasts and volunteers.

At Basford Bridge, a short detour from the towpath leads to Cheddleton Station **D**. The North Staffordshire Railway Society, based here, plan to operate steam trains between Cheddleton and Froghall. Currently, these fiery leviathans are confined to a short section of track at

▲ *The wooded Churnet Valley is a peaceful, unspoiled area today.*

the station. The neo-Gothic building is attributed to the Victorian architect Pugin, best known for his work on the Houses of Parliament.

The walk now follows the wide, flat valley of the Churnet to Oakmeadow Ford Lock **E**, where canal and river join forces at the start of a long, winding gorge.

A little way downstream, the remains of two limekilns **F** are all but hidden in the encroaching woods. Here, limestone from

The Flint Mill

There has been a mill at the point of the Churnet where South Mill now stands since the 13th century. Originally a corn mill, then a fulling mill, it was converted to grind flint in around 1800. Another mill, North Mill, had been built beside the same mill stream 40 years earlier for the same purpose. Both survive miraculously intact, their twin undershot wheels working a panoply of machinery dedicated to producing raw materials for the potters in nearby Stoke-on-Trent.

Flint is an important ingredient in the manufacture of fine china and porcelain, to which it gives both strength and whiteness. It is found predominantly in the chalk hills and downs of south-east England; a long journey by coaster and then by

The Flint Mill, which is still powered by water, can be seen in operation, crushing flint for the potteries at Stoke-on-Trent, at weekends and on some afternoons during the week.

narrowboat brought the flint to the canalside at Cheddleton.

There, it was first roasted, then crushed, before being mixed with water and ground to fine powder in the mills. The resultant, soup-like 'slop' was allowed to settle before being dried in a slip kiln, formed into blocks and sent by narrowboat to the potteries. All this occurred on this very compact site, interconnected by

a piateway and a series of pumps worked by the waterwheels.

Dedicated volunteers ensure that the mills are fully operational. South Mill also houses machinery for the crushing of various metallic ores, which give the potter a vast choice of colour to decorate their wares with before glazing. The old miller's cottage adjoining South Mill houses artefacts from centuries past.

ALL PHOTOS: JASON SMALLEY

▲ *Winding between wooded hills and farmland, the Churnet is a place to spot the common sandpiper, a small wader.*

Cauldon was roasted to rid it of impurities, before being transported on a horse-drawn tramway to Weston Coyney, about 7 miles (11.2km) away, and sold for fertilizer, whitewash and many other uses. The grassy track bed of the tramway can be seen disappearing up a wooded side valley above the kilns.

Two signposts, one metal, one sandstone, record the respective canal mileages to Uttoxeter and

Froghall. Etruria, also mentioned on the mileposts, is the junction of the Caldon with the Trent and Mersey.

FIERY FURNACES

Peaceful Consallforge **G** was once one of the main industrial centres of the upper Churnet. Iron ore and limestone were combined in furnaces to produce pig iron. This was transferred by canal, rail or packhorse to Leek and other locations to be transformed into firegrates, domestic utensils and tinplate.

A great bank of kilns still stands beside the canal, while in Crowgutter Wood, south-east of the hamlet, there are tumbled, ivy-covered walls lost in the woodland. Until very recently, it was all but impossible to reach this spot by car, and most people still arrive by foot or boat, aiming for the characterful Black Lion Inn, which overlooks the lock where river and canal once again separate.

The walk leaves the towpath and enters Consall Wood **H**, an open-access nature reserve managed by the County Council and criss-crossed by waymarked trails. The reserve protects the habitat of dozens of species of birds. The steep, wooded valleys are thick with

▶ *As you near Cheddleton, there are sweeping views over the countryside.*

birch and ash woodland. Beneath the trees are small bricked- or fenced-off shafts, the remains of small-scale coalmining activity that occurred here sporadically over many centuries.

Despite the waymarks, many of the paths are little used and hard to distinguish. This is true, in particular, of those in Upper Ladypark Wood **J**. Between the woods and Consall village, there are extensive views across the rolling countryside to the distinctive range of The Roaches, north of Leek, and the conical shape of Shutlingsloe, south-east of Macclesfield.

Beyond Consall, the route follows field paths through farmland, then follows the opposite bank of the canal to that on the outward route, to return to Cheddleton.

GOING FOR A BURTON

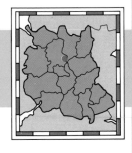

21

STAFFORDSHIRE

◄ *This splendid 19th-century bridge spans the River Trent at a point where there has long been a crossing. The wandering snail (inset) occurs in slow-moving waters such as the canal.*

SUE MORRIS. INSET: GEORGE BERNARD/NHPA

Discover the buildings and waterways of a famous brewing town

The all-pervading aroma of beer is the first thing that strikes the visitor to Burton upon Trent. Brewing has dominated this Staffordshire town for centuries, and the student of industrial history — as well as the beer enthusiast — will find much that is of interest here. In addition, some surprisingly green pockets remain, varying the scenery considerably in the compact area covered by this walk.

In the Middle Ages, the monks of Burton Abbey realized that the area's water, filtered through the local gypsum and rich in calcium and magnesium salts, was capable of producing excellent ale. Brewing continued in Burton after the abbey was dissolved. In 1744, William Worthington, a Leicestershire man, established a brewery in the High Street. William Bass did the same in 1777, and quickly established a reputation for fine quality beers.

Bass and Worthington were soon exporting their beers to the Baltic and Russia, and later to India. With the expansion of the railways in the 19th century, the Burton brewers began to exploit the home market, and beer became the national drink.

At the Bass Museum **Ⓐ**, where the walk starts, the visitor can learn all about the history and methods of brewing in Burton. Transport has always been an essential feature of the industry, and on display are early steam engines, vintage delivery vehicles and the Bass shire horses, which are still used to pull drays at shows and parades.

ROMAN WAY

The walk continues along busy streets. Derby Street follows the line of the Roman Ryknild Street (though it is difficult to picture this today), while Victoria Road is lined with 19th-century terraced cottages built for the brewery workers.

You turn off along the towpath of the Trent and Mersey Canal **Ⓑ**. Once busy with barges carrying cargoes of beer to the ports, the canal is now a leisure waterway. Colourful narrow boats glide along between the locks, and pleasure cruisers can be hired at

Shobnall Marina. The wild flowers by the water's edge, and the green expanse of Shobnall Fields opposite, provide a contrast with Burton's industrial face.

The route leads through St Paul's Square **Ⓒ**, now a conservation area, which was laid out following the building of St Paul's Church in 1874. The Gothic town hall was completed in 1894 by Michael Arthur Bass, the first Lord Burton. King Edward Place was created in 1906, after a visit by King Edward VII. Just around the corner in Wellington Street is a delightful row of almshouses, erected in 1875.

Some of the most significant buildings of Burton's industrial past line the next part of the route, which follows Borough Road and Station Street **Ⓓ**. The Midland Railway's

FACT FILE

- ☀ Burton upon Trent, 11 miles (17.6km) south-west of Derby, on the A38

- ⌗ Pathfinder 852 (SK 22/32), grid reference SK 249234

  miles 0 1 2 3 4 5 6 7 8 9 10 miles
  kms 0 1 2 3 4 5 6 7 8 9 10 11 12 13 14 15 kms

- ◔ Allow 2 hours

- ▬ Level pavements and easy footpaths throughout

- P At the start. Pay & display parking at Union Street and Meadowside Leisure Centre

- T / I Well served by trains and buses. For details, and tourist information, Tel. (01283) 516609

- 🍴 Numerous pubs, cafés and restaurants in Burton

- WC Bass Museum, main shopping centre, and Bridge Street

- 🏰 Bass Museum and Visitor Centre, Tel. (01283) 542031

THE WALK

BURTON UPON TRENT

The walk starts at the Bass Museum Ⓐ, in Horninglow Street.

1 From the main entrance to the museum, turn left along Horninglow Street. At the roundabout, turn left into Derby Street, and soon right into Victoria Road, which eventually becomes Dallow Road.

2 Just before the road crosses the canal Ⓑ, turn left down to the towpath. Continue, with the canal on your right, to Shobnall Marina. Walk up the steps to the road, and turn right (away from the canal).

3 Take the second left, Grange Street. Turn right down St Paul's Street. Walk around St Paul's

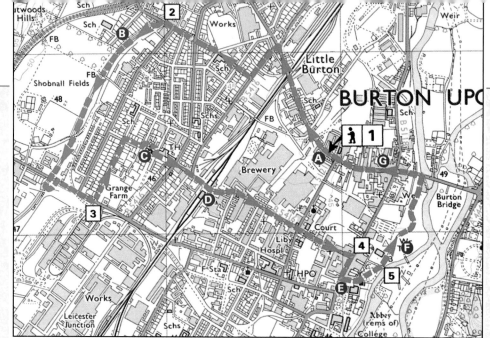

Square Ⓒ, and along King Edward Place, passing the town hall. Continue ahead across Wellington Street and down Borough Road, which becomes Station Street Ⓓ. Continue walking ahead, where the street is pedestrianized, to the High Street.

4 Turn right. At the Market Place Ⓔ, turn left. Go down the narrow lane to the left of the parish church. Take the path diagonally left across the Garden of Remembrance, towards the Washlands Town Park Ⓕ and the Andresey Bridge.

5 Just before the bridge, go through the gates on your left. Follow the path between the river and the town buildings to Burton Bridge. Climb to the bridge and turn left along Bridge Street, which becomes Horninglow Street Ⓖ, to return to the start.

Grain Warehouse No 2 was built in 1854. Now restored for use as offices, it retains the 'crimson lake and cream' livery of the railway in its paintwork.

Across the railway line is the impressive Ind Coope Brewery, built in 1859. The elegant stuccoed building a little further on is the Ind Coope offices, built in 1865.

The massive Bass No 2 Brewery, on your right, totally dominates the street. Inside the 3-foot (90-cm) thick walls is the famous Burton Union Room. Unions are containers in which fermentation of the beer is

▼ *These large barrels are unions for the final fermentation of beer. Behind them is the domed Magistrate's Court.*

completed. The room, nearly a mile (1.6km) in length, held 2,548 unions (averaging four barrels each).

The Market Place Ⓔ contains the Parish Church of St Modwen, which stands on the site of the Benedictine abbey. The present church dates from a rebuilding in 1719, and has many monuments to brewers inside. The Victorian Market Hall is impressive, and the weekly Thursday market, originally granted by King John in 1210, is still held.

Beyond the Market Place is a delightful green area by the River Trent, the Washlands Town Park Ⓕ. It is possible to explore the island in the Trent by crossing one of the footbridges. The holy water from a chalybeate well on the island once

attracted many pilgrims to Burton.

The large watertower on the left was built in 1856 to store quantities of the precious Burton water, drawn up from wells for brewing. Further on, by the weir, is an impressive 32-arch bridge, built in 1864 to replace a medieval bridge. Burton has long been a strategic crossing point over the Trent. During the Civil War, Cavaliers and Roundheads fought almost incessantly for possession of the bridge, and Burton changed hands five times.

BRIDGE STREET

The last part of the route leads along Bridge Street and Horninglow Street Ⓖ. The Burton Bridge Brewery is one of a new wave of small breweries, and produces five different traditional cask beers.

Nunneley House was built in 1760 by Samuel Sketchley, and later occupied by Joseph Nunneley's brewery. The early 18th-century house nearby was Charles Leeson's brewery from 1753-1800. A number of other fine 18th-century houses, many of which are sadly in need of restoration, line the street on the way back to the Bass Museum.

SUE MORRIS

IRONBRIDGE GORGE

22

An area of Britain's industrial heritage in spectacular scenery

▲ *The elegant structure of the world's oldest cast-iron bridge spans the Severn in Shropshire. Built by Abraham Darby III in 1779 the ribs (below) were cast in the blast furnace in Coalbrookdale.*

Ironbridge Gorge has been designated as a world heritage site for the wealth of attractions and sights that it has to offer. It is known as the birthplace of the industrial revolution, which occurred due to the fortuitous combination of coal, iron, transport and water power.

The iron industry of the area was closely associated with the Darby family and their firm, the Coalbrookdale Company. The name of the valley is derived from the graceful structure of the world's first iron bridge that spans the River Severn. Ironbridge itself is perched on limestone cliffs in the middle of magnificent Shropshire countryside. The area is uniquely preserved as it has remained almost totally undeveloped for over a hundred years.

RIVER DEE

Until the last 100,000 years, what is now the upper Severn basin in Shropshire and mid-Wales drained north, joining the River Dee and flowing into the Irish Sea. However, during the Ice Age this route was blocked and a great lake built up. The water eventually spilled over the hills to the south to reach a tributary of the River Stour and the lower Severn valley. As a result, the modern Severn turns away from the

---

FACT FILE

- ✳ Museum of the River and Visitor Centre, Ironbridge, Shropshire

- ▭ Pathfinder 890 (SJ 60/70); grid reference SJ 667036

  miles 0 1 2 3 4 5 6 7 8 9 10 miles
  kms 0 1 2 3 4 5 6 7 8 9 10 11 12 13 14 15 kms

- ◐ 3-4 hours for the longer walk; 1½-2 hours for the shorter route. You should allow plenty of extra time for visiting the museums

- ▬ Mostly easy walking but with some woodland sections that may be muddy after rain, so walking shoes are recommended

- P At the start of the walk. There is another large car park at Blist's Hill

- ⑪ Tourist office, cafés and restaurants in Ironbridge; ten pubs along route; Dancing Clowns Café at Jackfield Mill

- WC At start of walk and at Coalport Museum

- I Individual or family 'passport' tickets are valid for one admission to each museum. The museums are run by the Ironbridge Forge Museum Trust. Guidebooks are available

THE WALK

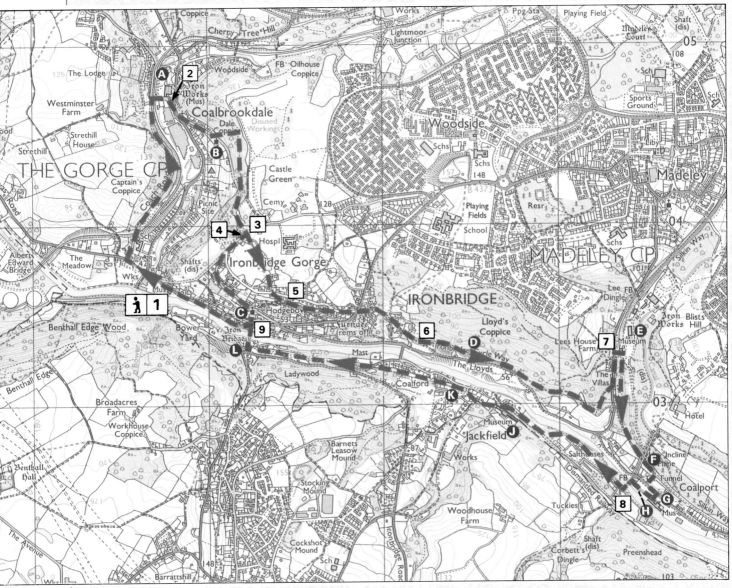

IRONBRIDGE GORGE

The walk begins at the exit from the Visitor Centre's car park, Museum of the River, Ironbridge.

1 Turn left along road for 200 yards (183 metres), then right up Station Road. Follow road over rise, take right fork down hill, then at 'Give Way' sign turn sharp right under railway bridge. Pass entrance to Museum of Iron **A** on left, then uphill to main road.

2 Cross to Church Road opposite and go up this, passing working men's cottages until level with the church **B**, then left over stile into wood. Bear immediately left, then right up steps, but after first 40 steps, turn right on fairly level path through wood. Turn left on road and go over rise, passing White Horse pub.

3 Cross straight over road to a signed public footpath; when track veers away to left, continue forward alongside hedge on right, then cross a field down to a road. Turn left at junction for 30 yards (27 metres), then right into Belle Vue Road. Follow this as it narrows to a path and winds among houses, to reach a junction with a very high wall, topped by railings, above you and a fine open view over gorge to right.

4 For Coalbrookdale short walk, turn sharp right and go downhill to meet St Luke's Road. Turn left at Ironbridge Church **C** for 20 yards (18 metres), then right down steps through tunnel under church and descend to Ironbridge. Turn sharp right to rejoin main route at Stage 9 back to the starting point.

5 Continue forward and slightly uphill, ignoring next turn to left, then carry on level section. At T-junction turn right onto Belmont Road. Keep right and downhill; cross main road taking great care as it is very busy with limited vision — use mirror on opposite post. Then go down footway opposite, to right of building with tower. Keep to left of Golden Ball public house, then turn right at junction to pass car park behind pub. After 100 yards (91 metres), fork right and downhill; 30 yards (27 metres) later, follow road around to left; walk along the level section for 200 yards (183 metres). Ignore track coming in from left, but shortly after bear left on track towards cottage in clearing.

6 Keep to right of cottage and garden hedge, then go up steep bank (the path appears faint at this point as it is overgrown) and across clearing, following power lines. At end of clearing, turn half-left into wood and ascend first flight of steps, then fork right up further steps to another clearing. Keep right of noticeboard **D** and

cross to far side. Pass sunken pool on left, then soon go straight on at junction of paths. The path winds through wood for some distance, dropping slightly; at times it is indistinct — occasional wooden steps confirm route. Turn left on path coming up from right, following edge of wood, which eventually swings sharply left and becomes a track leading to road. Turn uphill for 200 yards (183 metres), then half-right across parking area to 'Tradesman's Entrance', but just before this turn half-left downhill, and left again down steps.

7 Turn right for Blist's Hill Open Air Museum **E**.

Turn left into short tunnel. Keep on Silkin Trail until 100 yards (91 metres) after going under bridge **F**, then turn right down steps by wooden marker posts. Cross road and turn left on path, then right at first entrance of Coalport china works **G** (to visit museum, continue along road). Just before canal bridge **H**, turn right down steps, then left over second bridge. Continue alongside canal to footbridge over Severn and cross.

8 Turn right on road (which becomes a path) alongside Jackfield Mill. At end of buildings continue forward, passing houses on right to reach riverside. Follow road uphill away

from river, but when road bends sharp left continue forward and downhill on track towards river, then uphill towards church. Follow road past church to emerge by Jackfield Tile Museum **J**, and turn right; at next junction, keep right and downhill. When road swings right through disused level crossing gates, continue straight on along former railway line **K** called Severn Valley Way. Follow this for almost 1 mile (1.6 km) to reach the car park, then exit from far right-hand corner and cross iron bridge **L**.

9 Once over the bridge, turn left alongside the river to return to the start of the walk.

▲*The Museum of the River is a visitor's centre and is an ideal starting point for an exploration of the area.*

flat plain of north Shropshire to flow south through a narrow gap in the south Shropshire hills at Ironbridge.

This long, 6-mile (9.6-km) walk starts at the Museum of the River. This is housed in a gothic warehouse built by the company to store finished goods before they were sent off down the Severn.

The exhibits provide a good introduction to the area as a whole in words, pictures and sound. From the museum, a back road leads up the side valley known as Coalbrookdale to the Museum of Iron **A**. This is the site of the original furnace where, in

1709, Abraham Darby first began to smelt iron ore using coke, instead of the traditional charcoal. Displays, models and exhibits trace the history of iron, and the railway line carries coal for the Ironbridge power station just up the gorge. The village of Coalbrookdale was created by the company and the walk passes working men's cottages and the church **B**, built in 1850-54 with money from the Darby family.

From Coalbrookdale, the walk climbs through woods and across a corner of the plateau that the gorge

▼*The Hay Inclined Plane was designed to raise canal boats from the River Severn to the Shropshire Canal.*

cuts through. It follows back alleys through the upper part of Ironbridge, with good views across the gorge and down to Ironbridge Church **C** and the Iron Bridge.

From Ironbridge, the path leads through woods above the river,

▼*Wooden steps lead through the woods at Lloyds Coppice where the old system of coppicing is being reintroduced.*

The Abraham Darbys

MANSELL COLLECTION

Abraham Darby I, a Quaker ironmaster, first successfully began to smelt iron ore commercially using coke, instead of the traditional charcoal, in 1709. At that time, the timber used to make charcoal was in extremely short supply. This enabled cheap iron to be mass produced for the first time — giving rise to a large-scale iron industry in the area. Among the innovations that were made in Coalbrookdale were the first iron rails, the first

'Coalbrookdale by Night' by de Loutherbourg, painted in 1801, shows a romanticized depiction of blast furnaces.

iron wheels and the first iron-framed buildings.

Darby's grandson, Abraham Darby III, enlarged the existing blast furnace to cast the ribs for the world's first iron bridge. When the bridge opened in 1779 Ironbridge Gorge was one of the world's major iron centres.

visit the candle maker's shop and watch candles being made.

Going on along the Silkin Trail, an old railway line, you pass under the Hay Inclined Plane **F**, which raised and lowered small boats to link the Shropshire canal to the river.

SHROPSHIRE CANAL

The Coalport china works **G** thrived in the 19th century, but closed in 1926 and is now a museum of porcelain making. A short section of the Shropshire Canal **H** leads to a bridge across the river. You then return to Ironbridge beside the Severn, passing the Jackfield Tile Museum **J** and following the route of the Severn Valley Railway **K**. Its restored southern section, between Bewdley and Bridgnorth, can be travelled upon. The walk ends by crossing the Iron Bridge itself **L** to reach the little square at the centre of Ironbridge, with

BOTH PHOTOS THE IRONBRIDGE GORGE MUSEUM

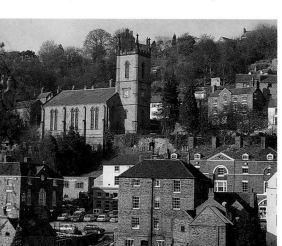

ROBERT EAMES

including an area **D** where the old system of 'coppicing' is being reinstated. The trees are cut back every 15 years to produce new young shoots. This coppiced timber provided materials for countryside items,

▶*This hand-painted plate is one of the collection of fine chinaware housed at Coalport. The historic town of Ironbridge (left) lies to the north as one stands on the iron bridge that gives the town its name.*

▲*Coalport China Works museum, with its distinctive bottle-shaped kilns, was once world famous for its fine porcelain. Now it is part of the Ironbridge industrial heritage trust.*

including baskets, hedge stakes and brooms. The woods also contain ruined industrial buildings.

You can then visit Blist's Hill Open Air Museum **E**, where many buildings from the district have been reconstructed to create a working industrial community — so you can

the church above, reached by climbing around a hundred steps.

The shorter walk of just 2½ miles covers the same ground as the long walk up to Stage 3 on the map. But this route takes in the Museum of Iron and also provides an excellent view of the Iron Bridge itself.

DEREK FORSS.INSET:ROBIN BUSH/NATURE PHOTOGRAPHERS LTD

▲The peaceful expanse of Cole Mere is one of seven meres in this area of Shropshire with a country park by the eastern shore. Water forget-me-not (inset) is paler than the garden variety.

Through farmland, alongside a canal and lakes rich in birdlife

Although this area is commonly known as the Shropshire Lake District, this is, strictly speaking, a misnomer. These expanses of water are meres — not lakes. Lakes have streams or rivers flowing in and out of them, meres do not. However, the word 'mere' is of Anglo Saxon origin and means 'lake'. Here they are referred to either as lakes or meres. This walk explores three of the largest meres and the abundant wildlife on their shores.

The group of meres at Ellesmere are the largest in the country and 'the Mere' is the greatest of these. It used to be much larger, surrounding the old town on three sides as a natural fortification. However, in 1805 the level was lowered artificially to allow the town to expand.

The walk begins at the Visitor Centre by the Mere **A**. The lakeside is usually well populated by many species of waterfowl. Mallards, coot and tufted duck mingle with Canada geese and black-headed gulls. The ground is bare due to the grazing birds. Out in the lake you will notice an island. The tree tops contain the large nests of the herons that return here each spring.

COW ISLAND

However, this island is not a natural feature. In 1812, the Duchess of Bridgewater undertook the task of terracing the gardens of Ellesmere House. This was done in the hard winter of that year, to provide work

▶ A half-timbered house in the small market town of Ellesmere that lies among farmland next to the meres.

in the town. The excavated soil was carted out onto the frozen mere and dumped, thus forming an island when the ice melted. In 1812 Napoleon retreated from Moscow and so the island acquired the name of Moscow Island, since abbreviated to Cow Island.

Cremorne Gardens **B** were given

FACT FILE

✳ Ellesmere, 8 miles (12 km) north-east of Oswestry. The Mere is on the east side of the town on the A528 to Shrewsbury

⊙S Pathfinders 827 (SJ 23/33) and 828 (SJ 43/53), grid reference SJ 404347

miles 0 1 2 3 4 5 6 7 8 9 10 miles
kms 0 1 2 3 4 5 6 7 8 9 10 11 12 13 14 15 kms

◑ Allow 4 hours

▬ Almost completely flat, only short and easy climbs. Walking shoes are recommended. Some road walking

P Two car parks by the Mere. The Castle Fields car park opposite the 'Boat House' is closed in winter

🍴 By the Mere in summer and in Ellesmere otherwise

🍺 White Hart, Black Lion, Red Lion and Ellesmere Hotel in Ellesmere all provide food

WC Near car park at the start

JOHN WATNEY

THE WALK

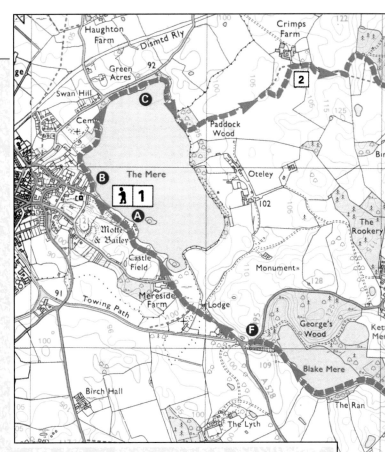

ELLESMERE – WELSHAMPTON – COLE MERE – ELLESMERE

The walk begins at the car park adjacent to the Mere Ⓐ.

➡ Follow the lakeside path towards Ellesmere. As you near the church enter Cremorne Gardens Ⓑ. Follow the lakeside path around the Mere passing a small island Ⓒ, known as Neddy Jebb's Island. At the other side of the lake, the path crosses three stiles. The third marks the end of the lakeside path. Immediately after crossing this, turn left and follow the fence and hedge on your left. (This can be overgrown with rape in summer months.) Cross a stile and continue with the hedge on your left to another fence. The path shown on the O.S. map has been re-routed. Turn right along this wire fence to the corner of a small field and then left towards Crimps Farm. The top strand of wire is electrified to contain cattle. Go through a galvanized gate into a lane.

➡ Turn right along this lane for about 300 yards (275 metres) until it ends at a white gate. This path has also been re-routed, so turn left around the field and up to a derelict house by the top corner. Continue along a waymarked path between a fence and some woods. From the next gate follow the marked path initially, but as it bears right, branch off left, at a tangent, to a stile in a fence. Cross the next field, heading towards the right-hand side of a small wood, to find a gate in the top corner of the field. Cross the stile, with the fence to the right and pass along the left-hand side of a pond. Continue and pass a small mere (fenced) also on the right. Keeping the fence on your right, go ahead to a gate into a lane.

➡ Follow this lane to a farm and the A495. (Take care on this stretch of road as there is no footpath and the traffic is fast.) Turn right along the road for 300 yards (275 metres). Just past the second cottage on the left, take a

JOHN WATNEY

◀ *The eastern shoreline of Cole Mere with Yell Woods, now managed as a conservation area, in the distance.*

collapsed into Church Street. The soil was removed, complete with skeletons, and was carted away by a man called Neddy Jebb. This work was done at night and the new island, which appeared in the Mere, has since been known as Neddy Jebb's Island. The channel separating it is kept clear to provide a haven for nesting birds.

WATER BREAKING

This corner of the Mere is shallow and is a popular feeding place for coot, mute swans and heron. On any of the meres you may notice the surface 'breaking'. This local term refers to the fermentation process in a brewer's vat. The mineral-rich waters and summer warmth combine to encourage the growth of algae. This floats to the surface and

to public use in 1953 by Lord Brownlow. The gardens had been laid out in 1855, when the last of the tanneries that used to be on the lake shore closed down.

You continue around the corner of the Mere, past the outflow grille that maintains the water at the new level set in 1805. Near the landing stage, a grove of beech trees with two giant sequoia is to be found. These grow to 300 feet (90 metres), and can live for 3,000 years. In the summer evenings this area is populated by bats hunting small insects. The pipistrelle, long-eared and noctule bat have all been seen.

You soon approach the Mere's other island Ⓒ. This is also man-made. In 1846 the churchyard

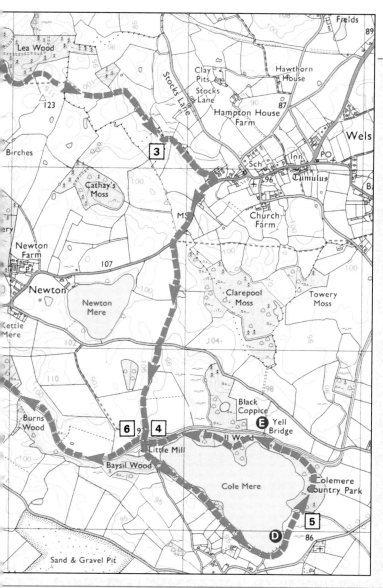

left turn into a lane marked 'Unsuitable for Motors'. Follow this for ⅝ mile (1 km) crossing a minor road, until it comes to a canal.

4 Cross the canal bridge and follow the lane past a house until you come to a gate turning left into 'Boathouse Wood'. This path now continues around the edge of Cole Mere passing the boathouse and sailing club to open grassland and its exposed shoreline **D** where there is a picnic area. Cross this to a gate to Yell Wood. (The woods around Cole Mere are managed as a conservation area and footpaths through the woods do not allow access to the water edge.)

5 A clear path goes through the wood to join the canal towpath. Follow this left to Yell Bridge **E**. It then goes back into the wood and continues

straight through to some canal-side buildings. These are workshops and stables by Bridge 55, which you crossed earlier. Go through the gate onto the road and cross back over the bridge to the towpath going to the left down a steep bank.

6 Follow this towpath, with the canal on your left, to Blake Mere. Here the path goes along a narrow spit of land between the mere and the canal. At the far end of Blake Mere follow the towpath through the tunnel **F**. At the other end turn right immediately to climb to the road. The exit from the canal towpath leads onto the A495, and care needs to be taken crossing to the footpath on the far side as approaching drivers are not aware of the exit until pedestrians appear. Follow the road left, returning you to the starting point.

Nature Walk

The course of CANALS can be used to estimate their age. Older canals took the flattest possible route that was often a snaking course.

Canals built later were cut straighter, as engineering became more sophisticated and tunnels and locks were built.

causes the appearance described.

Continue to Crimp's field where the path turns away from the Mere. Look back at a splendid view of the town across the water.

As you cross the farmland of the next stage of the walk, see how the land undulates due to the moraines deposited over the area by glaciers 12,000 years ago. Look out for other small meres that cover the Shropshire and Cheshire plains.

COLOURED PEBBLES

As Cole Mere is approached, a bridge over the canal takes you to Little Mill. A lakeside path goes through a plantation of Douglas Fir and Norway Spruce dating back to 1965. Continue round the lake to an exposed shoreline **D**. Notice the variety of colours of pebbles placed

▶ *This path is sandwiched between secluded Blake Mere, with its extensive wildlife, and the Shropshire Canal.*

here by the glaciers of 12,000 years ago. The pink ones are local sandstone, but the dark-blue are slates from North Wales, while the paler speckled ones are granites from Scotland or the Lake District.

St John's Church is built of sandstone and dates from 1870. Here, on

The Making of the Meres

As the last Ice Age was coming to an end — about 12,000 years ago — glaciers from Scotland, the Lake District and North Wales were converging upon the Shropshire and Cheshire plain, and melting. The rocks, sand and, most importantly, the boulder clay that had been scoured from other areas was deposited on the plain in large

quantities. This process possibly continued for centuries and the moraines (debris) left behind are extensive. Huge ice blocks had been pressed down into the clay and so when the ice finally disappeared the surface of the plain was undulating and pock marked.

Some of these pits are steep-sided and are known as kettle holes. They became filled with water and, even today, thousands of 'puddles' are spread over the area. Most have no stream or river flowing in or out, yet they remain filled with water because of the underlying water table which is only a few feet below the ground. Water, carrying nutrients with it, seeps up through the clay and so the meres have an abundance of plant, fish and other wildlife. The formation and natural maintenance of lakes in this way is unique in Britain and rare throughout the world.

With an area of 116 acres (50 hectares), the Mere is the largest of the waters at Ellesmere. Herons nest in the trees.

▲*The exit from the tunnel over the section of canal built between 1793 and 1805 by the engineer Thomas Telford.*

direct road access and no right of way to the far bank. Consequently it is a haven for wildlife. Fish, particularly pike, perch and bream, are abundant. These attract heron and kingfisher. The sheltered setting also attracts insects that, in turn, bring warblers, swallows and martins. The opposite bank is a private estate covered with woodland of sycamore, oak and Scots pine bordered by rhododendron.

BRONZE AGE SITE

You leave Blake Mere by entering the cutting to the tunnel ❻. From here to Llangollen the tunnels all have a towpath through them, which is unusual. As you return to the Mere notice the sandy hillocks to the right of the road. This is a glacial moraine deposited on the clay. It is well drained and was once covered by oak trees. These dry sites close to water and fish attracted early man and so it is not surprising that a Bronze Age canoe was found in the area.

the grassland, are Canada geese, joined by snow geese and barnacle geese in the winter.

The route now takes you through Cole Mere Country Park, which is largely situated on a narrow stretch of land between Cole Mere and the Shropshire Union Canal. The initials S.U.C. may be found on a boundary marker. You will soon approach Yell Bridge ❺. Notice the iron door in the bridge side. This is a storage cavity for some beams that can be placed across this narrow section of canal, in the slots provided, in order to form a dam. A drainage sluice is nearby so the canal can be drained prior to repair work.

As Little Mill is approached again, some canal-side buildings will be found. These were workshops and stables for the horses that towed the barges. Another boundary stone may also be found in this area, but with the initials of

▶*Yell Bridge crosses the Shropshire canal. The cavity stores beams used to dam the canal during repair work.*

E. C. The Ellesmere Canal Company linked the Shropshire Canal through to Llangollen. One of the main cargoes was limestone from Llangollen and limekilns can also be found near here. The limestone was heated to produce lime which was then used to dress the local fields.

The canal towpath is now followed to Blake Mere which is much more secluded, having no

SHROPSHIRE

From a town rich in architectural history to explore hills and valleys

Ludlow has often been described as the perfect historic town, which is not surprising once you become familiar with its treasures. Sitting astride a limestone outcrop, defended on three sides by the Rivers Teme and Corve, is a Norman castle, accompanied by its walled town. Streets, planned many centuries ago, are laid out in a rectangular grid in which is found a wealth of medieval, Tudor and Georgian architecture, including 469 listed buildings. The old name for the town was Ludelaue, meaning 'loud hill' or 'the hill by the loud waters', for then there were rapids rather than weirs in the river.

This walk begins by touring part of the town. It then goes out into the Mortimer Forest to visit features of the limestone anticline, or fold, responsible for the natural defences of the town. On the return there are panoramic views of these hills.

FACT FILE

- ✳ Ludlow, 10 miles (16 km) north of Leominster

- ⊡ Pathfinder 951 (SO 47/57), grid reference SO 517746

  miles 0 1 2 3 4 5 6 7 8 9 10 miles
  kms 0 1 2 3 4 5 6 7 8 9 10 11 12 13 14 15 kms

- ◔ Allow 4 hours

- ◼ Undulating country with one steady climb. Boots are advisable in wet weather. Not suitable for buggies

- P Free car park in Ludlow

- T BR line between Shrewsbury and Hereford

- 🍴 All facilities available in Ludlow

- P At the car park at the start and near Ludlow Castle

- ⌶ Ludlow Castle is open daily in April-September from 10.30am to 5.00pm, and in October-November and February-March from 10.30am to 4.00pm. There is an admission charge

▲ *From its great Norman tower there is a good view of Ludlow Castle, which was founded in the 11th century by Roger de Lacy. The oak bush-cricket (inset) can be seen in Mortimer Forest.*

Finally, the walk visits some more of Ludlow's ancient treasures.

The formation of Ludlow's environment began some 420 million years ago, when the sediments that formed the surrounding limestones and shales were first laid down on a

▼ *Dinham Bridge was built in 1823. It has three main arches and a smaller one for a mill-race running from the weir.*

THE WALK

LUDLOW – MARY KNOLL VALLEY

The walk begins at the free car park in Ludlow

1 Turn left out of the car park up to the town centre. Bear left by Gateways store and then right at the crossroads to see the Feathers Hotel. Enter the courtyard of the Bull Hotel, opposite, and walk through and up the steps at the rear. Go round the church and leave by the Hosyers Almshouses. Turn left by Ludlow Museum and go round the Butter Cross to the right and carry on to the market square and the castle **A**.

2 To the right of the castle entrance is a footpath going round the outside of the walls. Follow this round and down to where the path forks. Take the lower path, right, down to a road and Dinham Bridge **B**. Cross the bridge and follow the road right. Ignore a right fork and follow the road round a sweeping left bend. Soon the road turns sharp left but turn right into a 'No Through Road' towards Deepwood Farm.

3 After 70 yards (65 metres) there is a narrow path branching off to the left, climbing through the woods, to a road near the entrance to North Farm. Then turn left for 30 yards (25 metres). (If the path is overgrown go back up the main road to bypass it). Do not turn into the farm drive but follow a lane to the right. After 30 yards (25 metres) bear left up a stepped bridleway, keeping the field fence close on your left. After you pass through a tall gate the fence to the field swings away to the left and the bridleway forks. Take the right branch into the wood. Climb until you meet a forestry road.

4 Across this road is a path beside a sunken track. Follow this path (marked by red-topped posts) until it runs into the sunken track. Continue along this until it comes to fields on the left. Carry on by the edge of these fields to a lane that leads through the woods to a gate. Enter this field, keeping to the left past a barn, then turn left through a gate behind Mary Knoll House.

5 The lane goes down the hillside to another gate and then diagonally across

▲ *Walking through the woods in the hills is a delight at any time, but especially so in the spring and summer.*

▲ *Through Mary Knoll Valley, the route follows a wide, open track between coniferous trees. The view of Ludlow (below) from Whitcliffe allows you to admire buildings from many centuries.*

prehistoric sea bed. Corals, bivalve shells, early fish and shrimp-like creatures were trapped at this stage and their fossilized remains can be found today. The rocks were folded up as land masses moved.

The anticline that this formed is seen today as a high and wide range of hills that slope down and taper to a rounded point. The tip of this point has now been isolated from the remainder by the River Teme. This rocky outcrop supports the town and, across the river, to the south-west, the hills rise behind Whitcliffe. These natural defences were a perfect site for a castle when the Norman invaders needed to secure the borders with Wales.

As time advanced and needs changed, the castle expanded into a walled town, growing wealthy on the wool and cloth produced in the area. Many highly ornate, timber-framed buildings resulted from this early prosperity. Farm produce and the town's role as an administrative centre for Wales and the Marches ensured continuing wealth. In Georgian times Ludlow even became a fashionable resort.

Industry, using the waters of the Teme and the Corve, gave the town a sound financial base. In the 19th century, however, improved communications and the demise of its industries led to an exodus of the rich. There was little new development and the town retained its architectural magnificence, unsullied by Victorian 'improvements'.

LISTED BUILDINGS

The first of the magnificent buildings encountered on the walk is the Feathers Hotel. An earlier building was enlarged in 1619 and the following year it was opened as a hotel. It is one of the best known of all half-timbered buildings, with its beautifully carved exterior and an equally impressive interior.

The walk crosses to the courtyard of the Bull Hotel, no longer echoing to horses' hooves and iron-rimmed wheels, and climbs the steps to the churchyard. The Reader's House on the left is a medieval house that was rebuilt in 1555, with a porch added in 1616. St Lawrence's Parish Church was rebuilt from 1433 to 1471 but stands on original

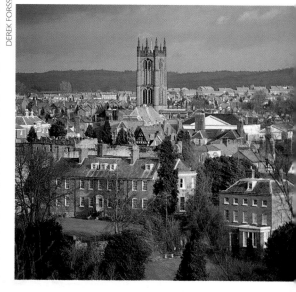

a field to Mary Knoll Valley **C**. Follow the track down the valley for 1 mile (1.6 km). It narrows to a path and then meets another track later, but continue, keeping the stream on your right. After passing a pond take a right fork by a cottage. The track crosses the stream. Keep the stream on your left and follow it to the village of Overton. At the road turn left for 200 yards (180 metres) past the entrance to Moor Park School.

➤ Shortly, turn left into a tarmac lane past the

entrance to a large house. The lane becomes stony and then meets another tarmac lane crossing it. Continue straight on along a grassy track through a gate. Follow the hedge, keeping it on your right, through two fields. You then come to an old gate that you cross. The hedge is now on your left. Continue in this direction to find a grassy track skirting the next field. You enter a farm lane and follow it past Hucksbarn to another field. This is skirted by following a

broken stone wall on the left. A stile leads to a path to the Overton Road.

➤ Turn left along the pavement towards Ludford Bridge **D**. Do not cross the bridge as there is a worthwhile detour. Turn left and climb the steps by Whitcliffe Lodge Cottage. Keep to the upper path and you come to a fine view of the castle and the town from Whitcliffe **E**, before descending to Dinham Bridge.

➤ Cross the bridge and go straight on to pass the

Chapel of St Thomas. Turn sharp right down a passage behind the chapel. At the bottom, turn left and follow the lane to Mill Gate. Note the medieval Great House over the road. Now go up Mill Street and turn right into Bell Lane and on to Broad Street. Down the hill, the 13th-century Broad Gate **F** still survives; up the hill is the town centre. Make your way up to the centre crossroads and turn right to find Tower Street, and return from there to the car park.

12th-century foundations. The Hosyers Almshouses were rebuilt in 1758. The Butter Cross is of a similar period (1743-6) but Bodenham's dates back to the early 15th century, when overhanging upper floors gave more space without encroaching upon the crowded streets.

Moving on towards the market square, look for Harp Passage with its cobbled paving, central gutter and overhanging upper storeys, giving the feel of a medieval street.

At the gate of the castle **Ⓐ** you can either go in and see the views from the tower, or turn right and go around below the ramparts. The path drops down to Dinham Bridge **Ⓑ**. The present structure replaced a medieval bridge in 1823.

THE FOREST

The route now moves on to the woodlands of Mortimer Forest. Incidentally, the name will not be found on any map as it is a collective name chosen by the Forestry Commission to cover many woodland areas in the vicinity. The walk climbs a steady gradient up above Whitcliffe **Ⓔ**, against the tilt of the folded anticline. The forest is a mix of broadleaved and coniferous trees, mainly oak and ash with some

▲ *The Feathers Hotel was originally the home of a council attorney called Rees Jones. It became an inn in 1670.*

planted beech, alongside Douglas fir, larch, sitka spruce and Scots pine. A herd of unique, long-haired fallow deer lives here and you may spot them if you are unobtrusive.

At Mary Knoll House the path begins the descent into Mary Knoll Valley **Ⓒ**. This deep, steep-sided valley was formed by a fault across the anticline, caused by untold stresses during the folding of the rock. Erosion of a ready-made line of

drainage has accentuated the feature. Bare rock faces may be worth examining for fossils.

The return walk crosses farmland to arrive at Ludford Bridge **Ⓓ**, built in the 14th century. Rather than cross the bridge, you turn left up the Wigmore road to gain a footpath over Whitcliffe. This affords one of the best-known views in Shropshire, looking across the Teme to the castle and the ancient town. The walk descends to Dinham Bridge and crosses it to St Thomas's Chapel, built around 1180.

MEDIEVAL SITES

Further on, at Mill Gate, there are good views of the town wall. Notice Palmer's Hall, belonging to Ludlow College. It used to be a medieval Great House. The walk climbs Mill Street to turn right into Bell Lane and through to Broad Street. Downhill is the 13th-century Broad Gate **Ⓕ**, capped by a 16th- and 17th-century house. As you walk up Broad Street to the centre there are several houses with blue plaques.

This tour of the town is merely a taste to whet the appetite. Guide books and guided tours are available if you wish to know more about this 'perfect historic town'.

JONATHAN PLANT

Ludlow Castle

DEREK FORSS

The building of Ludlow Castle began around the end of the 11th century. No timber castle preceded it and the original structure, comprising the inner ward, was built of limestone. Gilbert de Lacy was probably responsible for adding the large outer ward between 1160 and 1180.

In 1306, Roger Mortimer owned Ludlow and, by marriage, added vast estates to his own. He was behind the murder of Edward II and, for three years, Ludlow was the palace of the man who, in all but name, was King of England. He added the extensive range of buildings within the inner

Many different styles of architecture are incorporated in the buildings of Ludlow Castle, each a chapter in its long history.

ward. Edward III took his revenge and Roger Mortimer was hung, drawn and quartered.

By 1470, Wales was almost totally ruled by Edward IV. In an attempt to achieve unity he gave the Welsh their own ruler, his infant son, the Prince of Wales. The boy and his brother were sent to Ludlow. After their father's death, 11 years later, they were probably murdered by their uncle, Richard III.

The castle thrived until the Civil War but was surrendered to Cromwell in 1646. It fell into disuse and, in 1771, a survey concluded that the cost of demolition would exceed the scrap value. The Earl of Powys bought the castle in 1811 and its future preservation was assured.

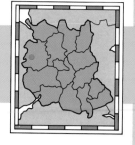

THE LONG MYND

From a market town in a lush valley to high grouse moors

Shropshire is a county of contrasts, combining quiet, prosperous farmlands with wild, windswept heights. This walk gives a taste of both. It begins at Church Stretton, a market town that became a holiday resort in the middle of the last century. The town lies on a valley floor that carries the road and rail links between the ancient towns of Ludlow and Shrewsbury.

The Romans recognized the importance of this valley to communications. A Roman road joining

FACT FILE

* ☀ Church Stretton, 12 miles (19.2km) south of Shrewsbury

* ⊡ Pathfinder 910 (SO 49/59), grid reference SO 453935

  miles 0 1 2 3 4 5 6 7 8 9 10 miles
  kms 0 1 2 3 4 5 6 7 8 9 10 11 12 13 14 15 kms

* ◔ Allow 3½ hours

* ▬ Difficult in wintry conditions. Mostly on footpaths through wooded valleys and over moorland. Long steady climbs, steep in places; over 1,000 feet (300m) of total ascent. Unsuitable for children. Walking boots advisable

* P Pay car park at start in town centre, or at Carding Mill Valley (free to National Trust members)

* T Frequent bus and train services running from Shrewsbury and Ludlow

* 🍴 Several pubs in Church Stretton, café in Carding Mill Valley open April-September

* WC At start and by information centre

* I There is a National Trust information centre in Carding Mill Valley

JONATHAN PLANT. INSET: D.N.DALTON/NHPA

▲*Cut into the slopes of The Long Mynd, steep-sided Townbrook Valley is part of the picturesque return section of the route. A wide variety of birdlife can be seen, including the wheatear (inset).*

Wroxeter and Leintwardine also runs through the town, and gives the place its name; Stretton is derived from 'Street Town'.

There are several other Strettons in the area. According to legend, they were inadvertently named by King Charles I on his way through the valley. He remarked, on entering a village, what a little place it was, and it became known as Little

Stretton. At the next town he commented on the attractive church, so naming Church Stretton. When told the next village was also Stretton, he exclaimed: 'It is all Stretton here!' and it was thenceforth All Stretton.

The church Charles admired, St Laurence, can still be seen at the start of the walk. There was a church here at the time of the *Domesday Book* (1086) and the nave dates from soon after that. Further work was done in the 13th and 14th centuries, which accounts for the fine medieval timber roofs. A carving of a Sheela-na-gig, a pagan female fertility symbol, can be seen on the

THE WALK

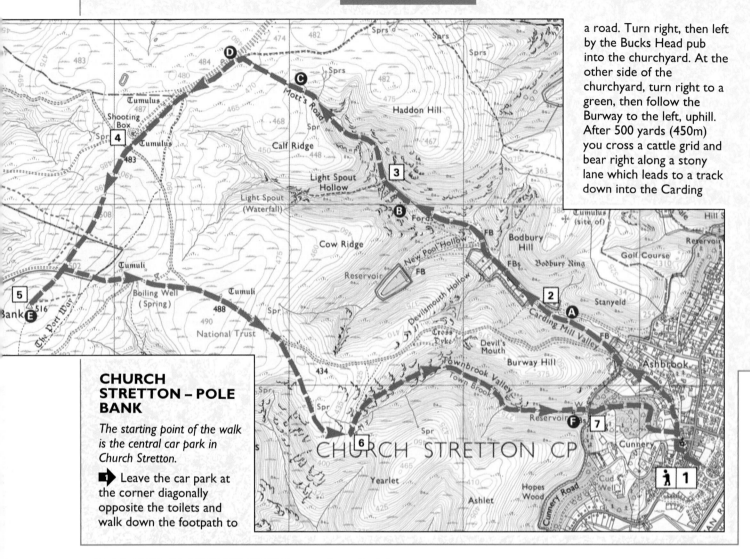

CHURCH STRETTON – POLE BANK

The starting point of the walk is the central car park in Church Stretton.

➡ Leave the car park at the corner diagonally opposite the toilets and walk down the footpath to

a road. Turn right, then left by the Bucks Head pub into the churchyard. At the other side of the churchyard, turn right to a green, then follow the Burway to the left, uphill. After 500 yards (450m) you cross a cattle grid and bear right along a stony lane which leads to a track down into the Carding

north wall of the nave.

From the churchyard you wind through the town towards the bulk of The Long Mynd, a range of hills occupying 70 square miles (181 square km). They are made of volcanic pre-Cambrian rock, the oldest rock to be found in England. The steep eastern edges of The Long Mynd are cut by a succession of deeply incised valleys, and the route goes up one of these.

Carding Mill Valley **Ⓐ** is a renowned beauty spot, now owned by the National Trust. It gets its name from a 19th-century wool mill, which replaced a flour mill that was already established here in the 15th century. The wool mill continued in business until earlier this century,

◀ *King Charles I once remarked on the charms of the Church of St Laurence in Church Stretton. The well-known beauty spot, Carding Mill Valley (right), is owned by the National Trust.*

BOTH PHOTOS: JONATHAN PLANT

Mill Valley Ⓐ.

▶2 Join the road coming in from your right and follow it ahead, past the National Trust Information Centre, to a stream. Cross it and follow a footpath upstream to rejoin the road above a ford. Continue past New Pool Hollow to the car park. Here, follow the path to the left of the main stream for nearly half a mile (700m), alongside the leat Ⓑ supplying water to the mill, to where two valleys meet.

▶3 Take the valley to the right and climb up Mott's Road Ⓒ. Keep on the main track out of the valley and across the moor to a signposted junction with The Port Way Ⓓ. Turn left towards Pole Bank, following a large clear track. Look out for some wooden posts on a bend in the track. Here go right, through the posts, and then left along a clear path which passes a ruined shooting box and then meets a road.

▶4 Cross the road and follow another clear path ahead. Cross a main track near some more short posts, and a short climb will take you to the summit of Pole Bank Ⓔ.

▶5 Retrace your steps to the track by the posts and turn right along this track down to a road. Turn left, then, at a T-junction, carry straight on. The road climbs and then descends steadily. There are a number of grassy parking areas to the left of the road. Near the end of these, to the right, is a clear track. Follow this to meet a stony track which bears to the left and ends at an open grassy area with two hillocks, marked by cairns, on the right. To the left of the second cairn a track leads down to a saddle with a hill in front of you and valleys to the left and right.

▶6 Descend the valley to the left on a path which crosses the head of the valley to descend diagonally down the left hand side to the valley bottom. Follow this valley all the way down to the reservoir Ⓕ.

▶7 Go through a kissing-gate into Old Rectory Woods. Cross the stream and climb some wooden steps. After a railed section of path bear left, downhill, at a fork. At another fork go right, uphill, and then left at a third fork (by a post marked '11'). Soon, turn right at a T-junction to find a stile on the left. A stepped path leads down and across a field to a road behind the church. Turn right to enter the churchyard on the left. Retrace your steps to return to the car park.

and was the centre of a thriving weaving industry, producing cloth and rugs. Its buildings have now been converted to residential use.

QUENCHING A THIRST

A tributary stream flows down from New Pool Hollow on the left. The reservoir constructed here in 1899, to meet the increased demands of the growing resort below, continued to fill this function until 1977.

Further up the valley, at the site of the upper car park, another mill pool possibly provided the original water supply to the first mill and later became a swimming pool.

A leat Ⓑ was built to divert the water from the occasionally unmanageable stream to the mill races, and traces of it remain in the valley. Just beyond this, a path along another tributary stream to the left leads to the waterfall of Light Spout.

Your route, though, takes you out of the valley by way of Mott's Road Ⓒ. The building of this track was financed by subscriptions raised by a Dr Mott, who wanted to improve access to some of his more isolated patients living in farms on the other side of the Mynd.

▼*Once a drover's road, The Port Way offers splendid views of the rolling hills to the east, including Caer Caradoc (right). The fort on its summit was once a defence against the invading Romans.*

DEREK FORSS

Mott's Road leads across bleak moorland covered with heather, bracken and bilberries. Up until the 1880s, bilberries were harvested by the poor of the district. In 1885 the crop was worth £600. The main harvest today is red grouse. Patches of heather are cut and burned in places to promote vigorous new growth because this is the favoured food of the birds. They were introduced into the area for sport in the 19th century.

Mott's Road meets The Port Way Ⓓ, an ancient track that was in use in the Bronze Age. It runs along the

JONATHAN PLANT

You carry straight on along the ridge to the summit of Pole Bank **E**, 1,693 feet (516m) above sea level. Here a toposcope points out such distant landmarks as the Brecon Beacons, Cadair Idris, the Malvern Hills and the Fiddlers Ferry power station on the Mersey, though you will need crystal-clear weather conditions to pick them all out.

From here you strike out across the moors, along a minor road and a footpath, to the head of Townbrook Valley, another of the steep-sided valleys cut into the slopes of The Long Mynd. This valley is home to a wide variety of birdlife. Pied wagtails and meadow pipits can be seen all year round, while wheatears, ring ouzels and spotted flycatchers are seasonal visitors.

A path leads through the valley by the brook. The reservoir **F** that sits at the bottom of the hollow was built in 1857 to supply Church Stretton, but it was soon superseded by the one in Carding Mill Valley. From the reservoir there is a short descent through the mixed woodland of Old Rectory Woods to the churchyard and back to the point where the walk began.

crest of a ridge that was once tree-covered. It was cleared over the years to provide grazing for cattle and sheep, and The Port Way became an important drovers' road.

Today, it provides fine views of the surrounding hills. The fort on the summit of Caer Caradoc, to the east, is supposed to have been the site of the last stand of the Celtic chieftain Caractacus in his fight against the Roman legions led by Ostorius Scapula in AD50.

▲*Beyond this cairn lies the descent into Townbrook Valley. Look out for snowdrops in springtime, during the short, pleasant walk through Old Rectory Woods (right), which is near the end of the route.*

BOTH PHOTOS: JONATHAN PLANT

Mary Webb

The novelist Mary Webb wrote that Shropshire was: 'A county where the dignity and beauty of ancient things lingers long.' It provides both the setting and the mood of her novels, in much the same way as Dorset was the inspiration for Thomas Hardy, Yorkshire for the Brontë sisters, and Cornwall for Daphne du Maurier.

She was born Gladys Meredith in 1881 at the lodge of Leighton Hall, 10 miles (16km) from Shrewsbury, the eldest of a family of six. In her teens she contracted Graves' disease, a thyroid disorder causing hyperactivity and, in her case, a disfiguring goitre.

In 1912, she married, and spent her honeymoon near Church Stretton, which she later fictionalized as Shepwardine. She and her husband Henry moved to Weston-super-Mare, but Mary could not settle, and they returned to Shropshire, renting Rose Cottage near Pontesbury, where she wrote her first novel, *The Golden Arrow*.

The book made no money. Henry was not earning enough to keep them both, so Mary regularly walked the 18-mile (29-km) round trip to Shrewsbury to sell produce from their garden.

Eventually, Henry found a teaching post in Cheshire and they moved to Chester. Again Mary could not settle,

Writer Mary Webb drew inspiration for her novels from the Shropshire countryside.

though she wrote *Gone to Earth* on weekend visits home. A job for Henry in Shrewsbury brought them back to Shropshire and a period of happiness, during which *The House in Dormer Forest* was written and published with a little more success than previous works.

However, her illness was progressing and her doctor advised a move to London where she could receive specialist care. There she wrote *Seven for a Secret* and her best-known work *Precious Bane*, published in 1925. This book, drawn from personal experience, concerns the suffering of a young girl caused by a deformity, a hare lip, and the ignorance and superstition of those around her. It was her last work; she died in October 1927, aged just 46. A few months later, the Prime Minister, Stanley Baldwin, praised *Precious Bane* at a literary luncheon and it became an immediate bestseller.

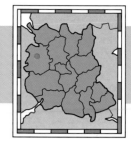

◀ *The first Tudor building you come to is Rowley's House, whose construction suggests it originally had an industrial use. The perch (inset) occurs in slow-moving sections of the Severn.*

FACT FILE

- ☀ Shrewsbury

- ⬚ 1:10,000 (SJ 41 SE), grid reference SJ 491129. A street map is recommended

  miles 0 1 2 3 4 5 6 7 8 9 10 miles
  kms 0 1 2 3 4 5 6 7 8 9 10 11 12 13 14 15 kms

- ◔ Allow 3 hours

- ▬ Mostly town walking. Suitable for all the family, though traffic can be heavy, especially on Saturdays. Sections along the river are muddy in winter

- P Frankwell pay and display car park at the start

- T BR Intercity; regular trains to and from the Midlands, Wales, London and the North-West

- ▦ Many pubs, restaurants and cafés in Shrewsbury

- WC Riverside Shopping Centre, Bear Steps, Coleham Bridge

- ⛫ Shrewsbury Castle and Rowley's House are open daily except on winter Sundays. For details of the abbey, Clive House Museum and Coleham Pumping Station, consult the Tourist Information Centre in The Square, Tel. (01743) 350761

A stroll in Shrewsbury, arguably England's finest Tudor town

The River Severn, swollen by rain from the Welsh mountains, loses its urgency when it reaches the Shropshire Plain. Any obstacle throws it into a meander. In Shrewsbury's case, the obstacle was a significant hill and the meander forms almost a complete circle.

The narrow neck of land that forms the break in this circle is reasonably high and easily defensible, making this an obvious site for a town. Possibly once a Welsh tribal capital, the town was certainly occupied by the Saxons, and by 1066 it was a significant town with five churches. After the invasion, it was fortified by Roger de Montgomery, the second richest and most powerful Norman after William I, who built a castle here.

FORTIFIED TOWN

The town and castle underwent further fortification until the Welsh were finally defeated, and Shrewsbury became a market town. It prospered in the Middle Ages and through into the reign of the Tudors.

Between 1560 and 1660, the town's population doubled. Much building work was undertaken, particularly of timber-framed mansions, and a good deal of the old town is still in evidence today. Besides the many fine buildings, there are ancient streets such as 'Doggepol' (today's Dogpole) and 'Le Wyle', both on record as early as 1246. Many interconnecting 'shuts' and passages, such as Grope Lane (1305), are also still in use.

The walk starts from the Frankwell car park, on the opposite bank of the Severn to the old town, and crosses the river at the Welsh Bridge **Ⓐ**. The present bridge was

THE WALK

SHREWSBURY

The walk starts in the Frankwell car park.

1 Go towards the river. Turn right along the bank to the Welsh Bridge **A**.

2 Cross and turn left to use the pelican crossing over Smithfield Road. Turn back to opposite the bridge, and then bear left into Hills Lane. Turn right to visit Rowley's House **B**. Return down Hills Lane, and go through the Victorian Shopping Arcade (opposite a car park) to the Mardol. Turn right to the entrance to Mardol Gardens opposite. Exit into Roushill.

3 Turn right to Roushill Bank, a pedestrian area, up past the entrance to Pride Hill Shopping Centre. This steep thoroughfare exits into Shoplatch. Turn left into Pride Hill's pedestrian area and carry on to Castle Street. Continue past Windsor Place on your right.

4 Turn left into School Gardens to pass the old school buildings **C**. Opposite Darwin's Statue, cross Castle Street to the half-timbered Castle Gates House and visit the castle **D**. Retrace your steps to Windsor Place. Enter Windsor Place and continue past St Mary's Church on your right and the Parade Shopping Arcade **E** on your left to St Mary's Court. This leads to Dogpole. Turn left and then right down a short alley by an estate agents into St Alkmund's Square. Turn right and go round the church **F** to Bear Steps Hall **G**. Exit by Bear Steps and Grope Lane to the High Street. Turn right then left into The Square.

5 Leave The Square by the narrow Coffee House Passage to the left of the Music Hall. Continue to College Hill and the Clive House Museum **H**. Turn left, then right along the path through the churchyard to Belmont. Turn left, then right into Belmont Bank. Beyond Sycamore House, bear left into Barracks Passage. This exits into Wyle Cop and Henry Tudor House **J**.

6 Go down Wyle Cop and over the English Bridge **K**, then continue straight ahead to the abbey **L**. Return to the English Bridge, but do not cross. Turn left to cross Rea Brook. Bear right to Longden Coleham, passing the Old Pumping House Museum **M**. At a pelican crossing, take a right turn to a footbridge back over the Severn. Turn immediately sharp left on a riverside path, and follow it for nearly 1 mile (1.6km) to the second bridge (a footbridge) back across the river. Cross to the Boathouse Inn. Turn right on a road, then right again into Water Lane. This returns you to the river. The riverside path goes under the Welsh Bridge to the Frankwell car park.

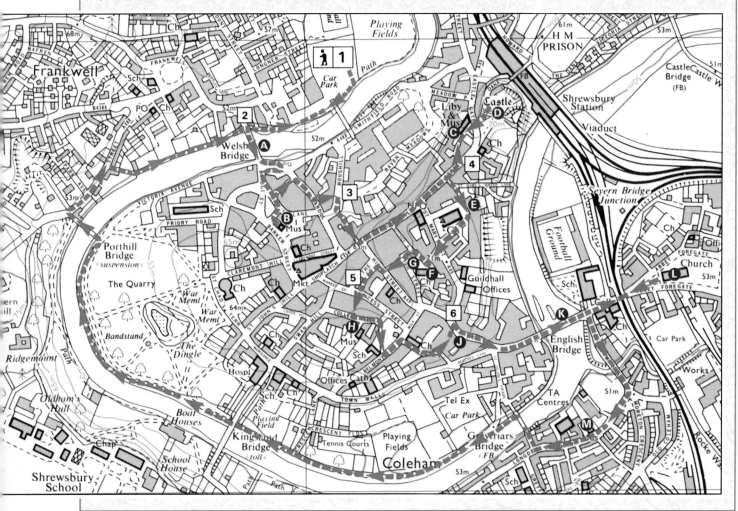

ALL PHOTOS: DEREK PRATT

◄*In front of the Old Grammar School, which now houses the town library, is a statue of its most famous old boy, Charles Darwin. Across the road is the 17th-century Castle Gates House (right).*

completed in 1795, but earlier versions date back to 1155.

The first significant building on this route is Rowley's House ❸, off Hill's Lane. Now a museum, it has displays of Roman artefacts from nearby Wroxeter, and exhibits on Shrewsbury's medieval past. The building dates from the 1590s. The absence of chimneys suggests that it was probably originally used for processing wool rather than as a house. The adjoining Rowley's Mansion, built soon after, is the earliest brick building in the town.

The route continues through the Victorian Arcade to the Mardol, where there is a late 15th-century inn, the King's Head.

In School Gardens are the old buildings ❸ of Shrewsbury School, which date from the 1590s, although the school was founded by Edward VI in 1552. By the end of the 19th century, the school had outgrown the buildings and moved to a site

across the river at Kingsland. One of its best-known pupils was Charles Darwin, who was born at The Mount, near the start of this walk. The route leaves his statue to cross the road to Castle Gates House, built in the 17th century in the Dogpole, but moved to this site in 1702.

The gateway survives of de Montgomery's original castle ❶, but the remainder is the result of rebuilding by Edward I. Restoration was carried out by Thomas Telford at the end of the 18th century, and it was he who built Laura's Tower, worth climbing for the view. The Shropshire Regimental Museum is now housed in the castle.

ROYAL CONNECTIONS

In Castle Street is the Old Council House, where the Council of the Welsh Marches met until its abolition in the Civil War. Charles I and James II both stayed here. In Windsor Place, the route passes the 16th-century Perches Mansion and the 18th-century Windsor House, before reaching St Mary's Place. The Royal Salop Infirmary of 1826 has been reborn as the Parade Shopping Arcade ❸. St Mary's Court leads to the ancient Dogpole, which you

▼*Shrewsbury Castle, built of red sandstone at the end of the 13th century and restored 500 years later, houses a military museum. The Bear Steps (right) are part of the medieval town.*

cross to reach the church ❻ in St Alkmund's Square.

The tower is medieval, but the remainder of the fabric was rebuilt in 1793-95. This may not have been strictly necessary, but Old St Chads in the town collapsed as the clock struck four one morning in 1788. This panicked the nervous church authorities into rebuilding St Alkmund's as well. In Butchers Row, off the square, is the Abbot's House, and shop fronts that are little changed since the 15th century.

Bear Steps Hall ❻, dating from the 14th century and recently restored by the Civic Society, now

▲*English Bridge, which crosses the Severn on the eastern side of the town, was widened for traffic in 1925.*

stages exhibitions. The actual Bear Steps lead into Grope Lane, named in 1324 when it was a dark and narrow passage. This area, more than any other, retains the feel of medieval Shrewsbury.

The Square became the focal point of the town in 1292, when the market was moved here. The Market Hall, built in 1595, reflects the town's prosperity in the Tudor period. On the inside of one of the columns at the north end of the hall are some pegholes, which were once used to record sales of fleeces. At the far end of The Square is the Music Hall, built in 1839; also of note are Wooleys House (1730) and the 16th-century Plough Inn.

Coffee House Passage, by the Music Hall, takes you through to the Clive House Museum ❶ on College Hill. Lord Clive, better known as Clive of India, lived in this house in 1762, when he was Mayor of Shrewsbury. The museum displays mostly porcelain and exhibits concerning life in the town during the 18th and 19th centuries.

Barracks Passage leads you to Wyle Cop, and Henry Tudor House ❶. Henry stayed here in August 1485 on his way to Bosworth, where he defeated Richard III and was crowned Henry VII on the battlefield. You pass Myttons Mansion and the Nag's Head Inn on the way to the English Bridge ❷, built in 1774, then dismantled and rebuilt in 1925 to widen the carriageway.

Gay Meadow, now Shrewsbury Town's football ground, is on your left. It is not unknown for the ball to be launched into the river during a game — on match days, one enterprising man patrols the river in a traditional coracle for the sole purpose of retrieving the ball.

BENEDICTINE MONASTERY

Just the other side of the bridge lies the abbey ❶. This Benedictine monastery, of which the Abbey Church is virtually all that remains today, was founded by Roger de Montgomery in 1080 on the site of a Saxon church. The refectory, cloisters and dormitory were once spread over the area where the main road now runs.

As you walk towards Coleham footbridge, you pass the Pumping Station ❶, which is now a museum. Its two large steam engines were built in 1900, and there are hopes of restoring them to full working order.

The return journey follows the riverside path around the outside of the town into The Quarry. The park is the site of an annual flower show. Standing in a commanding position at the top of the opposite bank is the main school building, originally a workhouse, of the present Shrewsbury School.

▼*The red-brick Coleham Pumping Station, built around the turn of the century, now houses a museum.*

Brother Cadfael

An illustration from A Rare Benedictine *shows Brother Cadfael conducting inquiries.*

No trip around Shrewsbury would be complete without some reference to Brother Cadfael. This fictional medieval sleuth is the creation of author and historian Edith Pargeter, who writes as Ellis Peters. She has given us a fascinating insight into life in 12th-century Shrewsbury.

Miss Pargeter was educated at Dawley and the County High School for Girls in Coalbrookdale. She began her working life as a chemist's assistant and joined the WRNS as a teleprinter operator in the war.

Her love for the area and her detailed historical knowlege of the period have combined to produce a credible character in a refreshingly different, but real setting. The Benedictine monasteries of the time held lands all over the country, and monastic business could take the brothers far and wide.

As a herbalist, Brother Cadfael had free licence to wander and to pursue his detective inclinations as he ministered to the sick away from his base in the abbey precincts. Much of the action, though, takes place around Shrewsbury itself.

The descriptions of places, and of the tension between the abbey and local people are based on fact; the abbey held the sole right for milling in the area until 1329, and this was a great bone of contention between the monks and the townsfolk.

Many of the places mentioned in this walk will be familiar to Cadfael fans, and details of a Cadfael Trail are available from the abbey, or from the Information Centre in The Square.

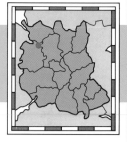

▲*Tyrley Locks, on the Shropshire Union Canal, are set in a wooded cutting through sandstone. The canary-shouldered thorn moth (left) flies in autumn in the woods.*

A stroll on a towpath and country lanes near a market town

There has been a settlement at Market Drayton since pre-Norman times, when it was known as Cair Draith Rut-Dan (Town on the Road). The *Domesday Book* refers to it as Draiture. Cistercian monks marketing their produce led to the town being granted a charter in 1245; since then, a market has been held here every Wednesday.

FIRE AND SPICE

A great fire destroyed much of the thatch and timber town in 1651. One survivor was The Crown Hotel. Charles I may have slept there in the Civil War; certainly his son, on becoming Charles II in 1660, ordered a nationwide collection to be made to rebuild the town.

The town's history since then is linked to the spice trade. Great stores of ginger, which at that time was second in importance only to pepper, were held here in the 17th century, and the town has been celebrated for its gingerbread since at least 1793, the first year a gingerbread maker was recorded there.

Market Drayton's most famous son was Robert Clive, who is better known as Clive of India. He left the town at the age of 17 to journey to India with the East India Company, who controlled the spice trade.

CANAL BOUNDARY

This walk starts at the edge of the town and explores the country to the south. You begin by making your way to the Shropshire Union Canal, which you join near an aqueduct, Berrisford Bridge Ⓐ. At this point, the waterway forms the county boundary with Staffordshire. The canal is on the top of a high embankment, reached by a flight of steps to the side of the aqueduct. As

SHROPSHIRE

JASON SMALLEY. INSET: NATURE PHOTOGRAPHERS

FACT FILE

☀ Market Drayton, 17 miles (27.2km) north-east of Shrewsbury, on the A529

🗺 Pathfinder 829 (SJ 63/73), grid reference SJ 675339

miles 0 1 2 3 4 5 6 7 8 9 10 miles
kms 0 1 2 3 4 5 6 7 8 9 10 11 12 13 14 15 kms

◔ Allow 2½ hours

▬ Mostly level walking on towpath, lanes and tracks

🅿 Car park off the A529 at the start

🇹 Regular buses from Newcastle-under-Lyme and from Shrewsbury

🍺 The Four Alls pub on the route.
🍴 Several pubs, restaurants and cafés in Market Drayton

🚾 At the start and at Tyrley Wharf

JASON SMALLEY

▲*The sign of The Four Alls pub, with a king, a general, a bishop and a citizen, explains the significance of its name.*

THE WALK

MARKET DRAYTON – THE FOUR ALLS

Start at the car park by the outdoor swimming pool at the bottom of Phoenix Bank.

From the car park entrance, turn left. Follow the road round, and up Phoenix Bank. Turn right into Great Hales Street and right again into Berrisford Road. Continue to the sandstone aqueduct **A**. Climb the steps up to the towpath, turn right and continue for just over a mile (1.6km), past Tyrley Locks **B**, to Tyrley Wharf **C**. Pass under the bridge and turn very sharp right to cross a stile onto the road. Turn left and follow it for ½ mile (800m) to the main road.

2 Cross and go down a minor road alongside The Four Alls pub. After ½ mile (800m), follow the road sharp right as a stony lane turns off to the left. Continue as the road becomes stony, past Salisbury Hill **D** on your left. The lane swings left, past a bungalow and a derelict house, to come to a T-junction.

3 Turn right and cross Walkmill Bridge **E**. At a T-junction, turn right and follow this road past the swimming pool to the start.

you walk along the towpath, the embankment gradually gives way to open farmland.

This peaceful stretch of water leads to a very attractive sandstone cutting in which are found the Tyrley Locks **B**. A canopy of trees casts deep shadows, creating a cool, moist environment in which ferns, mosses and liverworts thrive. The insects that enjoy such conditions are hunted by bats in the evenings.

COAL AND CHOCOLATE

At the fifth lock, you go under a bridge to Tyrley Wharf **C**. This was the point where the local Peatswood Estate loaded farm produce and unloaded coal. It was also used by the well known chocolate manufacturers, Cadburys, who collected the milk for their Knighton factory here. The buildings are dated 1837, and the lock cottage shows a strong Telford influence.

A quiet country road leads to The Four Alls public house, which dates back as far as the 16th century, though it has been extensively modernized. Its unusual name is derived from a King who rules all, a General who fights for all, a Bishop who prays for all and a Citizen who pays for all!

On the way back to Market Drayton, the route passes Salisbury Hill **D** away to the left. The Earl of Salisbury's Yorkist army camped here on their way to the battle of Bloreheath in the Wars of the Roses. Although heavily outnumbered by Lord Audley's 10,000 men, the men of the White Rose were victorious.

The lane emerges at Walkmill Bridge **E**, an old packhorse bridge on the outskirts of the town. It is a short walk from here back to the starting point of the walk.

▶ *The lock cottage and some of the neighbouring buildings date from 1837, when Tyrley Wharf was built.*

JASON SMALLEY

A canalside walk in Leicestershire

The great attraction of this canal walk is the combination of the quiet undulating countryside of south Leicestershire and the general activity of canal boats moving through the locks. Cut off from road traffic, there is complete freedom to walk along the towpaths and enjoy the special attractions that canals have to offer. Wildlife abounds around the canals, which provide a peaceful haven for birds such as mallards and moorhens — even the occasional kingfisher — and for small mammals such as the elusive water vole.

A FLIGHT OF LOCKS

Originally the canals were built to provide an essential network for carrying freight. Today they are plied by pleasure craft and narrowboats carrying numerous families on holiday.

Locks are an essential feature of canals, constructed to overcome the differences between water levels. Single locks are used where the change in level is slight, but a flight

DEREK PRATT / WATERWAYS PHOTO LIBRARY INSET S DALTON/NHPA

FACT FILE

- Foxton Locks, Foxton, Leicestershire

- Pathfinder 916 (SP 69/79) and 937 (SP 68/78), grid reference SP 692892

miles 0 1 2 3 4 5 6 7 8 9 10 miles
kms 0 1 2 3 4 5 6 7 8 9 10 11 12 13 14 15 kms

- Allow 2 hours

- Easy walk but take care of children near the canal. Ground may be muddy in bad weather, so good walking shoes are recommended

- **P** Car park just beyond Foxton village

- Picnic site near car park. Pub, café and shop near bottom lock

of locks is needed at Foxton where the gradient is steep. This walk includes the Foxton flight of ten narrow locks **Ⓐ** and the remains of Foxton Inclined Plane **Ⓑ** which was built to take boats up and down the steep hillside.

The flight forms one of the most remarkable features of Britain's canals. It was built between 1806 and 1814 as part of the Grand Union Canal's link across the Northamptonshire uplands to the Grand Junction Canal at Long Buckby. The flight was seen as a considerable engineering feat in raising or lowering vessels 75 feet (23 metres). However, passage through the locks was so slow — it took vessels over 70 minutes — that the locks became a bottleneck. As a result the inclined plane was designed to bypass the locks and save time.

▲ *Foxton flight with its two sets of five locks, viewed from the lock-keeper's house. The timid water vole (inset) eats the roots and stems of waterside plants.*
▼ *The striking yellow flag iris grows on the banks of canals and ponds.*

HEATHER ANGEL

THE WALK

FOXTON LOCKS – FOXTON

The walk begins at the car park and picnic site just beyond Foxton village.

1 From the car park turn left along the pedestrian way until you reach the canal. Pass under the road bridge, then over the canal by the new footbridge on to the towpath, with the canal now on your right. Walk down the towpath to reach the Keeper's Cottage and the top lock in the flight **A**. Cross the little footbridges to explore the inclined plane, engine house and small museum **B**.

2 At the bottom lock pass under the bridge and continue to the canal junction with the Market Harborough branch. Walk along the towpath, cross over the next bridge then walk down the towpath with the canal now on your left side. Follow the towpath northwards as far as Debdale Wharf (Bridge 65). Keep to the towpath; ignore the overgrown path on the right.

3 Retrace your steps the way you came. When you reach the point where the canal bends right, you have a choice of routes. You can return the way you came, back to the locks, or follow a bridleway across the fields to Foxton village. This route can be muddy and rutted in bad weather. For the bridleway follow instructions **4–7** below.

4 At the bend in the canal, turn left up a little path which ascends steeply up the embankment to join the bridleway at the top. Follow the bridleway round the left-hand side of the field, then bear right along the far edge of the same field, still keeping the hedge on your left, to reach the marker post where the hedge ends.

5 From the marker post walk directly across the field towards a telegraph pole (with red brick buildings behind it) and the large metal gates by the lane. If the field has been ploughed or cropped, follow the horse tracks down to the small stream, turn left then follow the bank of the stream to reach the gates.

6 On reaching the lane, turn right and walk along the lane to join the Main Street in Foxton village **C** by the canal bridge. Turn right over the bridge and go up the road past the church.

7 Continue along the road back to the car park at the starting point.

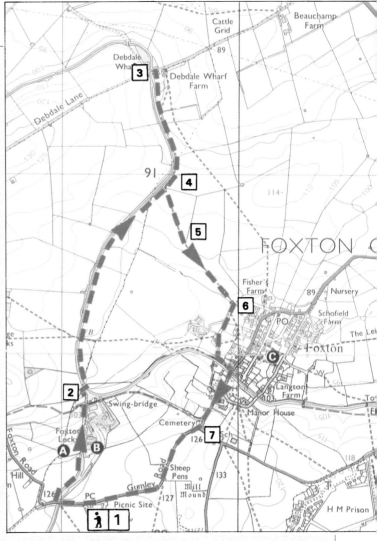

Sleepy Foxton, a picturesque village surrounded by fields.

THE INCLINED PLANE

At the turn of the century rails were laid in the side of the hill to take two baths or wheeled boxes full of water, each large enough to carry two narrow boats. They were counter-balanced so that the ascending bath was lifted by the weight of its descending partner. The system took only 12 minutes but it was expensive to run and by about 1910, as canal traffic declined, the incline went out of use and was later dismantled. Now, however, restorers are planning to rebuild the plane and there is a small museum and reconstructed engine house for visitors to look at.

This lovely walk continues along the towpath towards Debdale Wharf. When this opened for trading in 1797, Derbyshire coal, an important fuel, was on sale at 11d (about 5p) per hundredweight.

THE VILLAGE SCENE

In contrast to the busy canal scene, a walk across the fields ends in the peaceful countryside village of Foxton. Nestling on either side of the Market Harborough arm of the Grand Union Canal, this area was once a favourite hunting ground of John of Gaunt. The brother of the Black Prince, John was once Lord of the Manor at Foxton **C** and the manor house can still be seen near St Andrew's Church. The church is mainly 13th- and 14th-century, although there are earlier features, such as a fine Norman font.

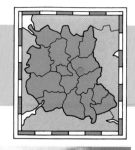

LEICESTERSHIRE

ALL PHOTOS MIKE WILLIAMS

From a deer park to one of the finest viewpoints in Leicestershire

This is an easy walk through a beautiful and historic deer park. It leads past the ruins of Bradgate House, the ancestral home of the Grey family, whose most famous and tragic member was Lady Jane Grey, queen of England for nine days in 1553. The walk ascends to one of the finest viewpoints in the county at Old John Tower, returning past volcanic outcrops of rock and through the ancient natural woodlands of Swithland with their disused slate pits and flooded quarries.

BRADGATE PARK

The walk commences in Bradgate Park **Ⓐ**, a deer park since early medieval times, which still contains herds of red and fallow deer. They are usually to be found in the south-west area of the Park. Bradgate Park has never been cultivated and retains its wild, open, heathland aspect. Its copses of ancient oak trees are probably some of the last remnants of the original Charnwood Forest, like Swithland Wood.

Both the House **Ⓑ** and Park are

The old chapel of Bradgate House.

▲ *Bradgate Park is an untouched stretch of moorland, woods, heath and rocky hills, covering 850 acres (343 hectares). (inset) Shy and secretive fallow deer roam the woods of the park.*

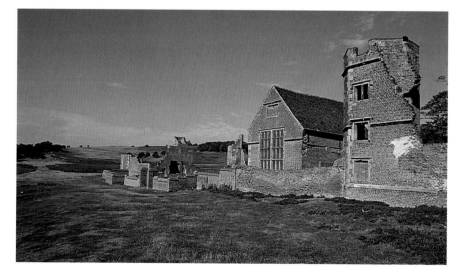

FACT FILE

⚐ Bradgate Park, near Cropston, Leicestershire

▭ Pathfinder 874 (SK 41/51), grid reference SK 542113

miles 0 1 2 3 4 5 6 7 8 9 10 miles
kms 0 1 2 3 4 5 6 7 8 9 10 11 12 13 14 15 kms

◔ Allow 2 hours

▬ Easy with one long hill climb. Woodland paths can be muddy after rain, so walking boots recommended

P Hallgates car park lies 6 miles (9.6 km) north-west of Leicester on the B5330 road near Cropston Reservoir, 5 miles (8 km) south-east of Junction 23 on the M1 motorway. The car park can be rather full on fine summer week-ends and Bank Holidays

WC At car park

THE WALK

HALLGATES - BRADGATE PARK- SWITHLAND WOOD

The walk begins at Hallgates car park near Cropston Reservoir.

1 From the car park, go through the large kissing gate and follow the tarmac drive for just over 1 mile (1.6 km) to reach the ruins of Bradgate House **B** in Bradgate Park **A**.

2 After exploring the site, take the broad path along the left side of the ruins, heading to the right of the wood. From the wood, follow the path upwards through a small copse and then up to Old John Tower **C**.

3 From the Tower, take the path that leads steeply downhill to the deer pond. Continue past the pond, on to the outcrop of rock called the Sliding Stone **D**.

4 Carry on down, keeping the plantation on your right-hand side, then

bear left to descend to the large kissing gate in the perimeter wall. Go through the gate and, ignoring the tracks to the right and left, cross the stile and follow the track ahead down to the road.

5 Cross the road (taking care because of the traffic) and enter Swithland Wood **E** through the gap in the wall. Follow the path straight into the wood for about 300 yards (270 metres), keeping in the same general direction, then turn sharp right along the broad track past the disused slate pits. The large, deep quarry pool is just to your left, and can be viewed safely from the perimeter fence. Continue past the pool to turn right on to the main bridle track which leads down to a small stream at the edge of the wood.

6 Turn left along by the stream to reach a stile and footbridge. Cross over

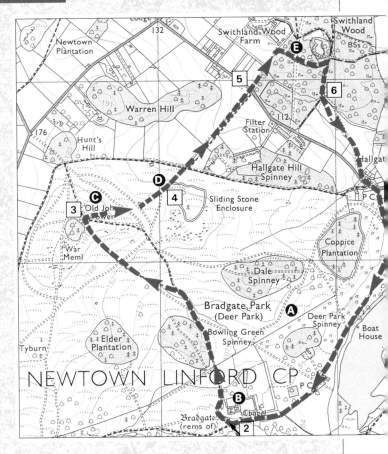

into the field and follow the path that runs diagonally across to the far right-hand corner by

the road. Cross over the road (with care at this sharp bend) to return to the car park at Hallgates.

---

forever associated with the Grey family, for many centuries one of the great noble families of England. Lady Jane Grey was born here in 1537. Unfortunately, she became an unwilling pawn in the Court intrigues of the day and, following the death of King Edward VI in 1553, she was placed on the throne by her scheming father-in-law, the evil Duke of Northumberland. Her reign lasted only nine days, and in a counter-plot, the 16-year-old girl was deposed and beheaded on the orders of Mary Tudor.

In the 18th century the House became increasingly unused, was badly damaged by fire, and eventually began to fall into ruins, so that now only the chapel remains intact.

OLD JOHN TOWER

Further on is an impressive Tower **C** that has connections with the Grey family. It was built in 1786 by the 5th Earl of Stamford, supposedly to commemorate the tragic, acciden-

Above Bradgate House is a late 18th-century folly—the tower of Old John, with views of Charnwood Forest.

tal death of the Earl's miller, 'Old John'. The tower was used for many years as a hunting lodge. It provides an excellent viewpoint across the Leicestershire countryside.

THE SLIDING STONE

From the tower there is a view of the Sliding Stone **D**. The granite outcrops of rock here and elsewhere in the Park are the result of volcanic activity about 700 million years ago, making them some of the oldest rocks in the country. Despite its name, the Sliding Stone has not been seen to move.

The walk ends in woods **E** that are very old, another remnant of the original Charnwood Forest. They contain disused slate pits and flooded quarries. The slate, quarried since Roman times, was widely used throughout the country for roofing and tombstones.

BURROUGH HILL

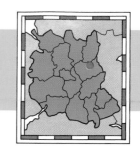

From an Iron Age hillfort, over hills and vales, to a quiet hamlet

This pleasant walk starts from an imposing and prominent Iron Age hillfort at Burrough Hill **A** that commands fine views over the gentle, undulating hills and vales of a quiet, rural corner of the county.

This area also lays claim to the origins of Stilton cheese, which is still made locally. The route includes the sleepy hamlet of Little Dalby with its beautifully situated church, built of the local mellow ironstone.

The track from the car park at the start of the walk leads to the imposing hillfort on Burrough Hill. Its prominent ramparts date from about 200 BC and the fort was eventually abandoned about 400 AD. It has been claimed that this was the ancient capital of the Coritani people (a tribe in the East Midlands at that time) before the Romans came and settled at Ratae (the Roman name for what later became Leicestershire). Excavations around the east gateway have revealed a

▲ *Markings on the toposcope on Burrough Hill indicate view points. The musk thistle (inset) grows on dry chalky soils.*

◀ *The village of Little Dalby may have been the place where Stilton, king of English cheeses, was first made.*

	FACT FILE
✳	Burrough Hill, 5 miles (9km) south of Melton Mowbray
🗺	Pathfinder 875 (SK 61/71), grid reference SK 7611

miles 0 1 2 3 4 5 6 7 8 9 10 miles
kms 0 1 2 3 4 5 6 7 8 9 10 11 12 13 14 15 kms

◐	Allow 4 hours
▬	Easy with undulating hills and vales. Boots or wellingtons needed as some sections are very muddy. Not suitable for children
P	About 3/4 mile (1200 metres) from Burrough-on-the-Hill village. Leaving the B6047 at Twyford continue through Burrough-on the-Hill and along the Somerby road to reach the car park at the sharp right hand bend. Entrance is on the left. Admission charge
🍴	Picnic site at car park

hill by the wood, the church was constructed from local ironstone at great expense by the Victorian Hartopps. The church dominates the quiet hamlet, where time seems to stand still.

After leaving the village and walking along a lane you can see an attractive wild-fowl pool **D**, near the bend on the lane, that contains many mallards. There is a small lake in spinny further along so the site attracts many other species of wild-

◀ *The wild-fowl pool near Little Dalby is a haven for mallard. A glimpse inside the church in Burrough-on-the-Hill (below).*

cobbled road and the foundations of a gate house. Microliths (the distinctive, tiny flint blades of the Mesolithic hunter) have also been found here.

From the 16th-18th centuries, the fort was a well-known site for many popular sports. Great crowds thronged the ramparts to watch horse racing, running and wrestling in the large, flat inner area, which made a fine natural arena.

Today a toposcope at the western end indicates the main viewpoints. Burrough Hill Covert **B**, below the ramparts to the north, was planted

as a fox covert at the end of the last century. It contains a particularly fine variety of trees including beech, birch, elm, spruce, pine and larch.

THE QUIET HAMLET

In the sleepy village of Little Dalby **C** stands Little Dalby Hall. Local tradition claims that this may be the birthplace of Stilton cheese. The hall was the family seat of the Hartopp family for over 300 years and was largely rebuilt in the middle of the 19th century. Close to the hall is the church of St James which was built in 1850. Beautifully situated on the

The Story of Stilton Cheese

Although it is named after a village called Stilton on the old Great North Road in Cambridgeshire, this rich blue-veined cheese is very much a Leicestershire creation and originated here. The county historian John Nicholls recorded that it was first made at Little Dalby Hall by the housekeeper, Mrs Orton, in about 1820. However, a similar cheese known as Quenby Cheese was also being made nearby at Quenby Hall by Mary Beaumont. In addition, Mrs Paulet, a farmer's wife at Wymondham, has also been credited as the first maker of Stilton. Whoever created the celebrated cheese, it is certain that cheese

Blue Stilton must be made with full cream milk from English dairy herds in certain districts in Central England.

from the district was supplied to the landlord at the Bell Inn at Stilton, and as a result, the cheese became more widely known and earned the rather erroneous title of 'Stilton'.

To make a genuine Stilton is a difficult and subtle process and the finer production methods are still a closely guarded secret. The immature cheese is sold as white Stilton and is milder and more crumbly than the strongly-flavoured blue variety. Local producers have successfully safeguarded the brand name over the years — the name Stilton is protected by a trade mark that applies only to cheese made in certain Leicestershire villages, including Long Clawson near Melton Mowbray and others in Nottinghamshire and Derbyshire.

THE WALK

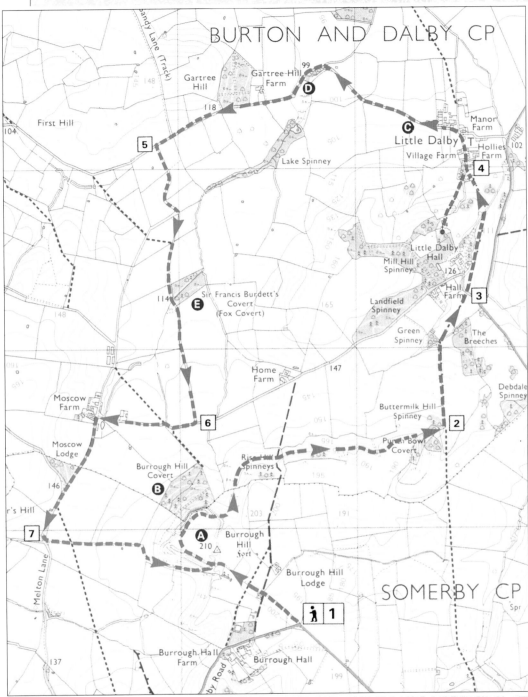

the left, near a little spinney, look for a yellow marker on a gatepost by the fence. Follow the path that bears right to the footbridge into the next field. Go diagonally across this field to reach the lane near the top left-hand corner.

▶3 Cross over the lane and go into the next field. Take a middle line across here to reach stiles and a footbridge that lead into a second field. Bear left over this field, crossing the drive up to the Hall, continue over the brow of the hill, and descend towards Little Dalby **C**, aiming for the gate just to the right of the first houses, to reach the lane.

▶4 If you wish to visit the church, turn left up the lane and then up the little tarmac path through the field. After visiting the church, retrace your steps and return to Little Dalby.

To continue the main walk, turn right down to the cross roads. Turn left and follow this lane for about 1¼ miles (2 km) (passing the wild-fowl pool **D**) until you reach a broad track on your left, about ¼ mile (400 metres) past Gartree Hill Wood. (Beware traffic.)

▶5 Turn down this track, which is an ancient 'green lane' (muddy in winter) and follow it for about 1 mile (1.6 km) to reach another lane, passing Sir Francis Burdett's Covert **E** on the way.

▶6 At the lane, turn right down to Moscow Farm. At the farm turn left and go up the lane for about ¼ mile (400 metres) to a road junction. Turn left and go down the road for about 150 yards (130 metres) to reach a junction of field tracks.

▶7 Turn left and follow track back to Burrough Hill.

BURROUGH HILL – LITTLE DALBY

The walk begins at the car park for Burrough Hill.

▶1 From the car park, follow the track ahead that leads straight on to the hill fort **A**, passing through three gates.

After you have fully explored the site and seen Burrough Hill Covert **B** below the ramparts, look for the yellow-topped marker posts to the north-east of the hill. These indicate the Dalby Hills concessionary path. This may be very muddy in winter and on very rare occasions may be closed to the public. Follow the way-marked route along the edge of the Dalby Hills, for just over a mile to Buttermilk Hill Spinney.

▶2 At the end of the Spinney, do not continue on the waymarked route into the field, but turn left to go down towards a gravel track between two fields. Where the track bends to

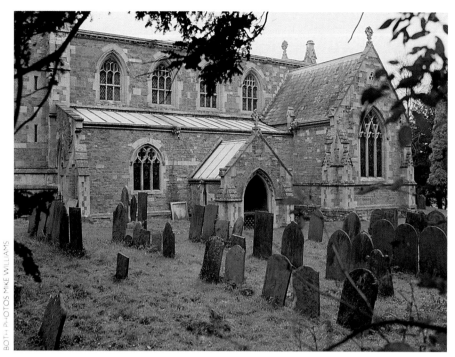

Fox hunting has been a 200-year-old tradition in this countryside and has significantly affected the landscape and social history. The many woods and spinneys were originally planted and maintained as fox coverts. Fields were kept small and in pasture, and bounded with low-cut blackthorn hedges to make jumping easier.

The many halls and country mansions in the area were built as hunting lodges. When hunting was at the height of its popularity and fashion

◄ *The 19th-century Church of St James stands on a hill outside Little Dalby. A carved detail (below) on the window arch.*

fowl. Further along the lane is a fox covert or small wood known as Sir Francis Burdett's Covert **E**. It was planted by and named after the radical politician who lived from 1770-1844 and hunted in the area in the 1820s. The covert has been carefully conserved and, like the Burrough Hill Covert, passed earlier on in the walk, Sir Francis Burdett's Covert contains a fine variety of trees. These coverts are attractive havens for wildlife and add to the pleasant countryside views surrounding Burrough Hill.

This area is very much the heart of Leicestershire fox-hunting country, the Burrough Hill ridge being the boundary between the Quorn Hunt territory to the west, the Cottesmore Hunt to the east and the Belvoir Hunt to the north.

in the 19th and early-20th centuries hundreds of riders, including British and European royalty and nobility, took part in the hunts.

Horses and hounds were carefully bred over the years and chases totalling 15 miles (24 km) or more over the then undulating grasslands were not uncommon.

Steeplechasing originated from the hunt when young gentry from Melton raced across the countryside from village church to village church, sometimes on moonlit nights and often for wagers.

In the breeding season adult rooks carry food to their young in a throat pouch.

Nature Walk

Churchyards are rich in reminders of the past that often reveal the age of the site. Here are a few examples to look out for in the churchyard:

LYCHGATE *A roofed churchyard gate where bearers waited with a coffin for the priest. Some date from medieval times.*

SPIRES AND TOWERS *The styles of these show when the church was built. They house the belfry and the church bells.*

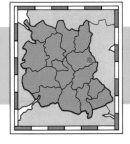
LEICESTERSHIRE

Exploring an inland peninsula that juts out into Rutland Water

This walk is a circuit around Hambleton Peninsula, a long finger of high ground almost surrounded by Rutland Water, a vast reservoir. The walking is mostly level and passes through a mixture of sheep pasture and woodland. You are never far from the Water, which is used by yachtsmen, windsurfers, a pleasure cruiser, anglers and a large number of waterfowl.

The walk begins at the village of Upper Hambleton **Ⓐ**, which clusters around Hambleton Hill, commanding views in all directions over the water. In Anglo-Saxon times, the

JANET HARRISON/AQUILA. INSET: AGENCE NATURE/NHPA

▲*The view from Armley Wood across Rutland Water, which is popular with birdwatchers, sailors and fishermen. The reservoir has been stocked with rainbow trout (inset) and brown trout.*

village was one of the capitals of Mercia, before being superseded in importance by nearby Oakham. According to the *Domesday Book*, Upper Hambleton, one of only four places in Rutland to be mentioned, had three churches in 1086.

The current church, dedicated to St Andrew, dates from the 12th century, but is built on earlier foundations. Much of the present building is Victorian, but it contains a 12th-century holy water stoup and coffin lids of a similar age. The 13th-

century tower has a broach spire.

From the village, a bridleway leads to a well-defined track which skirts the peninsula and is part of a 24-mile (38-km) walking and cycling circuit around Rutland Water **Ⓑ**. The Water is renowned for its fish, especially trout, and record catches have been made here.

GROWING TOWNS

The reservoir, created to meet the burgeoning demand for water from Milton Keynes, Northampton, Wellingborough, Daventry and Corby, was begun in 1971 and completed six years later.

The shallow Gwash Valley was dammed near Empingham. The dam wall **Ⓒ**, visible from the walk,

FACT FILE

- ☀ Upper Hambleton, 2½ miles (4km) east of Oakham, off the A606

- ▣ Pathfinder 896 (SK 80/90), grid reference SK 900076

  miles 0 1 2 3 4 5 6 7 8 9 10 miles
  kms 0 1 2 3 4 5 6 7 8 9 10 11 12 13 14 15 kms

- ◕ Allow 2¼ hours

- ▭ Short descent at start and gentle ascent at end, otherwise level walking through woodland and fields. Walking boots recommended

- Ⓟ By the road in Upper Hambleton

- ▦ Finches Arms, Upper Hambleton

THE WALK

UPPER HAMBLETON – BARNHILL CREEK

The walk begins at a road junction beside St Andrew's Church in Upper Hambleton village Ⓐ.

1 Walk along the village road eastwards for 100 yards (90m) to a footpath sign – a sole print – on your left. Turn left through the wooden gate and walk along the wide, hedged track to its end by a sheep pen. Go through the gate and descend the field, aiming towards the right-hand corner where there is a gate near a 10mph sign.

2 Walk down the track towards Rutland Water Ⓑ and follow it round to your right. After just over ½ mile (800m), enter Armley Wood. Continue on the track for another 1½ miles (2.4km), with the dam wall Ⓒ visible to the east, to reach Barnhill Creek.

3 At the creek, keep on the track and follow it away from the water. After about ¼ mile (400m), cross the road from Upper Hambleton and turn right along the parallel track. Normanton Church Ⓓ is visible behind you, across the water. When the track goes left, follow it down towards the water and Hinman's Spinney. Follow the track through the spinney to the fields. After ½ mile (800m) following field boundaries, you pass through Hambleton Wood. The path continues through more fields, with woodland to your right and Old Hall visible ahead.

4 Just before the drive to the hall, cross a stile to the right of the drive to Old Hall Cottage. Ascend the field to two stiles at the top and continue, with the field boundary on your right, to a gate. Keep on up the hill and you return to Upper Hambleton and St Andrew's Church.

is 1,312 yards (1,200m) long and 131 feet (40m) high.

The reservoir has a capacity of 27 billion gallons (120 billion litres), making it the largest man-made lake in western Europe. It takes its name from the former county of Rutland, of which Oakham was the county town. The county, the smallest in England at 152 square miles (394 square km), was absorbed into Leicestershire in 1974.

From the east end of the peninsula, there are views across to Normanton Church Ⓓ, which juts out into the water on a bed of rocks. Originally, it was to have been abandoned to the reservoir; monuments inside the church were moved to St Mary's at Edith Weston, and 180 bodies in the churchyard were exhumed and cremated. However, in 1972 a voluntary group succeeded in raising the £30,000 needed to build a bank and a causeway of stones to protect the church. It now houses a museum about the construction of Rutland Water.

MANY KINDS OF BIRD

The reservoir is a magnet for wildfowl and you will see mallard, swans, grey herons and many other birds as you follow the circuit back to the village. More than 200 different species have been sighted, including ospreys on migration and great northern divers in winter.

◀ Once an ordinary inland village, Upper Hambleton's well-maintained houses are now almost surrounded by water. Its hilltop location offers some fine views.

LEICESTERSHIRE

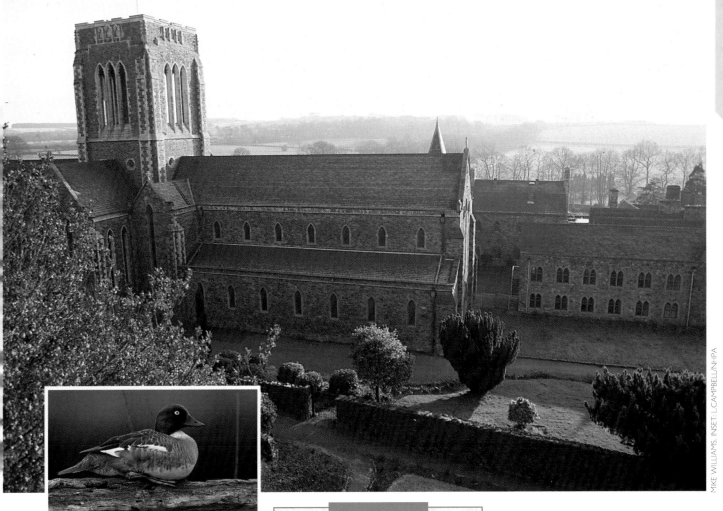

MIKE WILLIAMS. INSET: L.CAMPBELL/NHPA

A 19th-century monastery set near quiet water and woodland

This is an easy and delightful ramble through the north-west corner of the Charnwood Forest, an old deer-hunting preserve. The area is an oasis of tranquillity and beauty in the industrialized East Midlands.

SIMPLE GRANDEUR

The walk begins at the austerely beautiful Mount St Bernard Abbey Ⓐ. The church and the other monastic buildings — constructed from local granite in the Cistercian

FACT FILE

✳ Mount St Bernard Abbey, 5 miles (8km) south-west of Loughborough

🗺 Pathfinder 874 (SK 41/51), grid reference SK 458161

miles 0 1 2 3 4 5 6 7 8 9 10 miles
kms 0 1 2 3 4 5 6 7 8 9 10 11 12 13 14 15 kms

◖ 3 hours

▭ Good paths, tracks and lanes. Field paths may be muddy in wet weather

🅿 Car park at the start; monastery gates close at 7pm, or earlier in the winter

🍴 Gift shop and picnic area at the start

♿ WC At the start

▲*The buildings of Mount St Bernard Abbey, designed by Augustus Pugin, reflect the doctrines of the Cistercians, who espouse simple living. Goldeneye ducks (left) visit the nearby reservoir.*

tradition of solemnity and simplicity — were designed by the eminent Roman Catholic architect, Augustus Pugin, at the very beginning of his distinguished career. Building began in 1837 and took a century to complete. The abbey was eventually consecrated after the war, in 1945.

THE CALVARY

The nave of the church is usually open to visitors, who are also allowed to attend some of the monastic services. To the side of the church is an attractive, short, stepped climb through beautiful gardens. The focus of these gardens

THE WALK

MOUNT ST BERNARD ABBEY – BLACKBROOK RESERVOIR

The walk begins at the car park of Mount St Bernard Abbey Ⓐ, which is signposted from the A512 (junction 23 of the M1).

1 Walk back down the main entrance drive to the road. Turn right and walk for about 100 yards (90m) until you see a footpath sign on your left.

2 Turn left and follow a clearly waymarked path through a wood (this is part of the Charnwood Forest Geological Trail). Cross over three stiles and turn left onto a track leading down to Blackbrook Reservoir Ⓑ. Continue across a bridge over the reservoir and follow the track uphill to come to a road.

3 Turn left and follow the road for just over ½ mile (800m) to Fenney Windmill Ⓒ. A little way past this, just before a crossroads, a footpath is signposted on the left.

4 Cross a stile and follow the path diagonally over a field to reach a stone squeeze-stile. Go through this and turn left. Follow the lane to a bridge over the Black Brook.

5 Follow the waymarked path through a wood to a gate into a field. Turn left and follow a clearly-marked path around field edges. When you reach a lane, turn right and walk down to the crossroads at

Poacher's Corner.

6 Turn left and walk up the road past High Sharpley Ⓓ to a T-junction.

7 Turn left along Oaks Road. It is possible to follow this road back to the monastery, but the main route turns right at a footpath sign after about ¾ mile (1.2km).

8 Take the path across the right-hand corner of the field. At a stile, leave the waymarked path ahead and instead turn left along a grassy track, passing Whitlock Quarry Ⓔ, to come to a public viewing platform.

9 Take the left fork and then a waymarked path alongside a wall. Continue across gorse heathland then left along the side of a field to a drive.

10 Turn left and follow the drive back to the monastery's car park.

MIKE WILLIAMS

◄ *Begun over 150 years ago on land gifted to the Cistercians, the abbey's immaculately kept gardens are tended by the monks, who have made full use of Midlands granite when building its walls and steps.*

ALL PHOTOS: MIKE WILLIAMS

is a Calvary, a representation of Christ's Crucifixion, with the cross perched on a rocky mound.

Calvary (from the Latin word 'calvaria' meaning 'skull'), also known as Golgotha (the Aramaic word for 'skull') is mentioned in all four Gospels as being the name of the hill on which the Crucifixion took place, so called because of its skull-like shape. Alternatively, the name may derive not from its shape, but from the bones that would

▲*As the route leads across Blackbrook Reservoir, there are beautiful vistas through the trees and across the water.*

inevitably have been strewn around such a hill of execution.

The abbey gardens are usually open to the public, but the main buildings and grounds that belong to the monastery are private.

GEOLOGICAL TRAIL

On leaving the abbey, you go briefly down a lane before following part of the Charnwood Forest Geological Trail to Blackbrook Reservoir **Ⓑ**. The present reservoir was built in 1906 to supply drinking water to the growing urban areas of Loughborough and Shepshed. It was constructed on the site of a smaller, 18th-century feeder reservoir supplying the old Charnwood Canal.

MIGRANT BIRDS

A superb wildfowl habitat, the reservoir's permanent residents include Canada geese, coots, moorhens, mallard and great crested grebes. There is also a rich variety of migrants. During the winter months there are ducks such as goldeneye, teal and shoveler, and you may even

◄*Fenney Windmill has been beautifully renovated since the middle of this century, when it was in a state of decay. Further along the route is a squeeze-stile (right) built from the local granite.*

Nature Walk

By looking carefully at a fallen tree you can discover a lot of information about the length and quality of its former life. Look out for:

GROWTH RINGS These indicate the rate of growth: the wider the spacing, the better the growth.

RESIN BARRIER At some time in the tree's life, a resin barrier may be secreted under the bark to protect the tree from fungal attack.

RICHARD PHIPPS

111

▲ *A viewing area at Whitlock Quarry gives walkers the opportunity to watch operations at a working granite quarry.*

spot Bewick's and whooper swans that have flown in from Siberia and Iceland respectively.

Next, you come to Fenney Windmill **ⓒ**. The mill dates from the 1840s and was owned and worked by the local Draper family until 1935, when it was abandoned. It had fallen into considerable disrepair by the 1950s, when it was bought and restored as a private residence.

DRAMATIC OUTCROP

Lanes and good paths take you across fields, through woods and over Black Brook to Poacher's Corner, where there is an excellent view of High Sharpley ridge **ⓓ**, a dramatic granite outcrop designated a Site of Special Scientific Interest. The rocks are over 600 million years old and some are covered with rare lichens. The surrounding woods are haunted by foxes. There was once public access along the ridge, but this is no longer the case.

After you turn off the road onto a footpath, there are good views of Whitlock Quarry **ⓔ**, which has been considerably extended and deepened in recent years. Abbey Grange, on its edge, has been completely demolished and in its place is a viewing platform from which you can safely observe operations. Most of the granite that the quarry produces is used as hardcore for road-building.

From here, it is a short and pleasant walk across some fields and along a drive back to the abbey car park and the start of the walk.

The Monks of Charnwood

There is a long tradition of monasticism in Charnwood Forest. Until its enclosure in the mid-19th century, this was a wild and remote area that attracted religious orders and hermits who sought to withdraw from the outside world.

For over 400 years, there was an Augustinian Priory nearby at Ulverscroft, as well as a smaller community at Grace Dieu, even nearer to the present monastery — just 2 miles (3.2km) to the north-west. The ruins of both these medieval foundations can still be seen.

The monastic tradition was revived in 1835. A small group of

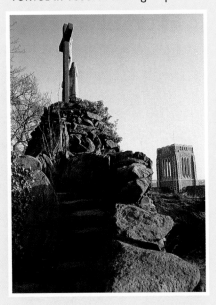

Cistercian monks founded a community in a cottage on the site of the present abbey, set in land given to them by Ambrose Philip de Lisle, an enthusiastic convert to Catholicism.

It was the first Roman Catholic monastic settlement to be founded in England since the Reformation (1534), at which time Henry VIII outlawed the Roman Catholic church and declared his own supremacy, with religious authority passing out of Rome and into the hands of the monarchy.

The monks at Charnwood set about clearing and cultivating the land, and work began on the present buildings. The community flourished and expanded. Many eminent Victorians, including Gladstone, Dickens and Florence Nightingale, came to visit what at that time was a unique institution.

The monastery became renowned for helping the poor, feeding many thousands, especially agricultural workers, during the hard times of the 19th century. It is still an active community, with about 40 monks leading an enclosed, contemplative life devoted to prayer and work. After a lengthy novitiate, the monks take vows of poverty, chastity and

The Calvary, situated at the highest point of the gardens, overlooks the abbey and provides a focus for the monks' reflections.

obedience, and also observe a vow of silence for much of the day, in keeping with the original spirit of the Cistercian order.

The Cistercians, who have also been known as 'white monks' or 'Bernardine monks', were founded in 1098 at Cîteaux in Burgundy. A group of Benedictine monks, led by Robert of Molesme, had become dissatisfied with what they saw as lax principles operating in their abbey. They set up a new order with the aim of living in solitude governed by a rigid observance of the Rule of St Benedict in its strictest form.

In the 12th century, St Bernard joined the foundation at Cîteaux, and by the time of his death the order had grown enormously under his influence, with 338 Cistercian abbeys in countries as diverse as Sweden, Scotland and Portugal, as well as the eastern Mediterranean.

Over the centuries the vehemence of their principles became somewhat diluted. In the 17th century, Armand-Jean Le Bouthillier de Rancé (1626-1700), the Abbot of La Trappe for more than 30 years, set about reinforcing the disciplines that Robert had instilled at Molesme. He enforced a regime of strict diets, punishing exercise and absolute silence. The name 'Trappist' came to describe those monks who observed vows of silence and lived in seclusion.

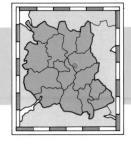

Walking to the site of the battle that ended the Wars of the Roses

The Battle of Bosworth Field on 22 August 1485 was one of the great turning points in English history. The death of King Richard III, and the defeat of his forces by those of Henry Tudor, ended the long, unstable period of the Wars of the Roses. This was achieved in an encounter that lasted only an hour, and took the form of brutal and clumsy hand-to-hand combat.

A PASTORAL CORONATION

This was the last occasion on which a King of England died fighting in battle. Henry was crowned Henry VII — it is said that the crown was found behind a bush while Richard's men were still being

FACT FILE

- ✳ Sutton Cheney, 4½ miles (7.2 km) north of Hinckley

- OS Pathfinders 894 (SK 40/50) and 915 (SP 49/59), grid reference SK 410004

  miles 0 1 2 3 4 5 6 7 8 9 10 miles
  kms 0 1 2 3 4 5 6 7 8 9 10 11 12 13 14 15 kms

- ◔ Allow at least 1½ hours

- ▭ Good paths, tracks and lanes, suitable for whole family; field paths and towpath can be muddy after rain

- P Car park in Cheney Lane; at start; or at Visitor Centre

- ¶ Pub in Sutton Cheney; restaurant at Visitor Centre

- I Visitor Centre open April-Oct. Several special events in summer, Tel. (01455) 290429

▲ *Though a peaceful agricultural scene today, Bosworth Field was once the scene of fierce hand-to-hand combat. Amphibious bistort (inset) grows nearby. At King Dick's Well (below), Richard supposedly took his last drink.*

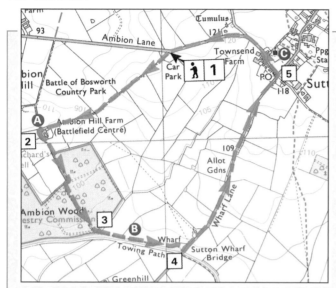

BOSWORTH FIELD – SUTTON CHENEY

The walk begins at the Cheney Lane car park.

1 With your back to the entrance of the car park, take the clearly waymarked path from the right-hand corner. Keep to the right of the next four fields to come to the Battlefield Visitor Centre **A**.

2 Take the waymarked path from the Centre to a stile on the other side of Ambion Wood.

3 Cross over the stile, and follow the path along the canal **B** to a car park and bridge at Sutton Wharf.

4 Turn left along Wharf Lane to Sutton Cheney **C**.

5 Take the first left, Ambion Lane, to return to the car park.

slaughtered, and was placed on Henry's head with the battle still raging. Henry established the Tudor dynasty, which brought prosperity and stability at home, as well as power and great conquests abroad, finally coming to an end in 1601, when Elizabeth I died without issue, and the throne passed to the Stuarts of Scotland.

This walk explores the site of the historic battle, now pleasant farm-land, and the country round about. It begins at the car park for the Visitor Centre **A**, near the hamlet of Sutton Cheney. Most of the actual fighting took place on Ambion Hill close to here, but the battle was named after the small town of

▼*Sutton Wharf, on the Ashby-de-la-Zouch Canal, is a pleasant spot to relax quietly and watch the boats drift by.*

Market Bosworth, which lies on the sky-line to the north. The excellent displays in the Visitor Centre are augmented by events throughout the summer, while the well laid out and very informative Battlefield Trail gives an account of the battle, and the events that led up to it.

ASHBY CANAL

From the Visitor Centre you walk through the conifers of Ambion Wood to the Ashby Canal **B**, which was built between 1794 and 1804 to transport coal from the developing coalfields in the north-west of the country to Hinckley and Leicester. It was never a very successful venture, and was superseded by the Leicester to Swannington Railway, one of the earliest lines to be built in Britain, in the 1830s.

Where the canal is crossed by a

▲*The delightful row of 17th-century almshouses in Sutton Cheney has been converted into tea-rooms, and can provide food and lodging for visitors.*

lane at Sutton Wharf, you turn up the quiet road to Sutton Cheney **C**. Richard III marched through here from Leicester with his troops, before camping out on Ambion Hill the night before the battle. The quaint 14th-century church was standing then, and tradition has it that he attended his last Mass here on the morning before the battle. To the east of the church, there is an attractive row of almshouses, founded in 1612, which have now been converted into tea-rooms.

Just outside the village, as you walk down another lane back to the car park, you pass an early Bronze Age burial mound. Richard is said to have addressed his forces at this ancient site on the eve of the battle.

BOTH PHOTOS: DEREK FORSS

A stroll among quiet lanes, woodlands and hedgerows

This walk begins in the lovely countryside to the south of the Birmingham conurbation. Here there is a fine network of quiet footpaths and lanes just waiting to be explored. This is an area where the views are constantly changing as hedgerows have not been torn down to create vast arable fields. The region is popular with Midlands businessmen seeking a respite from the daily grind and the route passes

FACT FILE

- Hockley Heath on A3400. About 12 miles (19 km) south-east from the centre of Birmingham

- Pathfinder 954 (SP 07/17) grid reference SP 152728

miles 0   1   2   3   4   5   6   7   8   9   10 miles
kms 0 1 2 3 4 5 6 7 8 9 10 11 12 13 14 15 kms

- 3 hours (allow extra time if visiting Packwood House)

- Mainly level terrain with gentle hills. Easy paths over pastureland — many are waymarked. Some lane walking. Boots are not necessary but stout shoes are recommended; wellingtons would be advisable in winter

- **P** Service roads off main road but take care not to block access. The Nag's head Inn on the corner of the A3400 and B4101 has a car park usable only during pub opening hours

- Inns and shops at Hockley Heath. Packwood House open April to end of September, Wed to Sun and Bank Holiday Mon (closed Good Friday) 2.00-6.00 pm; Oct, Wed to Sun 12.30-4.00 pm. There is an admission charge

- **WC** Toilets available at Packwood House

PAUL FELIX

F A JANES/NHPA

▲ *The undulating countryside of the fields at Packwood. Limited arable farming means that hedgerows, pesticide-free fields and horses' paddocks (left) encourage wildlife.*

by many large, impressive mansions with equally grand gardens.

The starting point is Hockley Heath on the A3400 (formerly the A34). There are many villages hereabouts with 'heath' in their names, signifying the gravelly nature of the soils in the settlements created in clearings in the vast and ancient forest of Arden. In days past the place was also known as Hockley

Port. There was a salt and general trade warehouse on the Stratford Canal behind the Wharf Inn.

Over the fields is the little church of Packwood Ⓐ which is dedicated to St Giles. There are many wood beams in the church that date from the 15th century, traces of a Norman wall painting and a 14th-century tower with a curious history.

MEDIEVAL MURDER

Nicholas Brome lived a few miles away at Baddesley Clinton. He found a priest 'chockinge his wife under ye chin' and promptly murdered him. The crime received a papal pardon; in expiation, Brome added towers to the churches at Baddesley and Packwood.

Almost 300 years ago Michael Johnson brought his bride Sara Ford to Packwood Church.

HOCKLEY HEATH – LAPWORTH

The walk starts from the junction of the main A3400 and the B4101 road at Hockley Heath.

➊ Walk along the B4101, which is signed to Knowle. Within ¼ mile (400 metres) the road bears right. A footpath is signed through a white metal kissing gate.

➋ Pass through a second kissing gate onto a drive and cross over. Keep ahead and follow a well-used path that crosses another drive. Keep ahead along a waymarked track to a meadow, staying beside a hedge on your left.

➌ Pass through a gap in the hedge and bear right from hedge to walk past a water trough that is situated in the middle of the field. Cross fence stile to road on right-hand side of the field.

➍ Turn left and walk

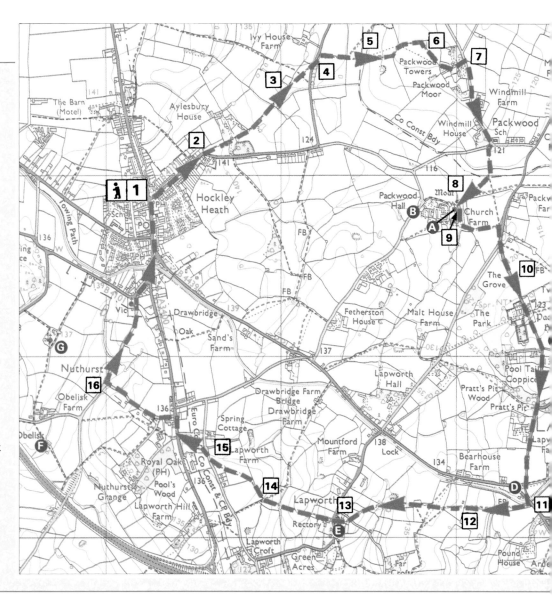

Three years later their son, the famous poet, essayist and critic, Samuel Johnson was born.

Opposite the church is an ancient moated house. The timber-framed Packwood Hall ❸ has fine chimneys and is of historic interest, but is not,

◄ *The tower of St Giles's church was built in expiation of the killing of a priest by the murderer.*

unfortunately, open to the public.

Packwood House ❸, on the other hand, is one of the most frequently visited properties in the Midland counties. It was thought to have started as a modest farmhouse in about 1560, but has been added to greatly over the centuries. The interior of the house is considered a fine example of Tudor domestic architecture. However, it is the garden that attracts the crowds.

The Yew Garden is mid-17th century in origin. It was the design of one John Fetherston and represents Christ preaching to the Multitude in the Sermon on the Mount. The clipped yews are said to take three men one month to prune.

Also well-known at Packwood are the elaborate sundials. There are half a dozen of them on the build-

▲ *The flower garden in its summer glory; it is situated at the south front of the half-timbered Packwood House.*

THE WALK

along the road a few steps. Cross road to a path signposted through a gateway (no gate). Walk along a wide track that crosses arable land and goes over a concrete bridge over a ditch.

5 On the far side of the field maintain the direction to climb the hill alongside the hedge. At top, path bears left and continues along a grassy track with hedge on left.

6 Follow hedge round top of the field to a fence stile by a metal gate (in top right-hand corner of field). Turn left into vehicle drive to a road. Turn right to arrive at Windmill Lane.

7 Bear right at T-junction and take path signposted over a fence stile. Walk straight across the field then go over a bridge and 'squeeze' stile. Turn half-right aiming towards a church tower.

8 Pass through a corner gap. Nearby there is a kissing gate to the churchyard of St. Giles's church **A**. The church is open. Opposite the tower is the moat of Packwood Hall **B**. Return to church entrance and take a wide grassy path that leads diagonally away towards the far left-hand corner of the churchyard.

9 Pass through a gate and, passing little Church Farm, turn left over rough pasture to a wide bridge across a brook. Turn left through a gateway (no gate). The path leads straight (old hedge line) to a road. Cross fence stile and turn right. This is Packwood Road, which becomes Packwood Lane at a junction.

10 The lane leads along a tree-bordered way and through pillars to Packwood House **C** with its magnificent yew garden. Go straight to the road junction. Maintain the direction — the lane is signed to Lapworth. At the next road junction bear left to the B4439.

11 Turn left over the Stratford Canal **D**. Take the footpath over a stile on the right. Walk the length of the pasture to pass through a hedge gap. Stay on the same bearing alongside hedges on the left to a cricket field.

12 Cross cricket field to top left-hand corner. Cross waymarked stile. Continue to second stile. Descend to muddy pool. Keeping pool on right, follow path carefully and ascend diagonally to left. Cross difficult stile. Go through small paddock and cross stile onto lane. Turn right to War Memorial, 20 yards (18.3 metres) further on.

13 Turn right, then left by war memorial to St Mary's Church **E**. Opposite the church climb over stile to a meadow. Descend the hillside to pass through a gate. Maintain the heading over the ridge and continue to a stile and bridge over a brook.

14 Climb out of the vale to a kissing gate and junction of pathways. Through the gate, turn right alongside the hedge. After 300 yards (274 metres) and in line with a row of trees (old hedge line) turn 45 degrees left across the pasture.

15 Continue to a kissing gate to lane. Turn right. At T-junction turn left, then right at main road. After a short distance turn left down lane.

16 The lane leads to a T-junction. You may be able to see the Archer obelisk **F** on the left and the lovely spire **G** straight ahead. Turn right. Climb the rise to a junction. Turn right along the main road then left to arrive back at the starting point.

◀ *The interior of Packwood House is notable for its fine collection of tapestries, needlework and furniture as is evident in the Long Gallery.*

ings and some are again the work of John Fetherston. The sundials bear Latin inscriptions such as 'Septem sine horis' (Seven without the hours) to remind us that in the summer the night is very short.

After crossing the Stratford Canal **D** the path goes over meadows and a cricket field to Lapworth Church **E**. This hilltop place of worship (St Mary the Virgin) dates from the 12th century and is unusual as its tower and spire are almost detached. The advowson (patron) of the church has been in the hands of Merton College, Oxford, for 700 years and over the centuries several graduates have become the rector.

Lapworth also produced one of the conspirators in the Gunpowder Plot. Robert Catesby, the chief originator, was thought to have been born at Bushwood Hall about 1573.

Over the main road the narrow lane twists uphill towards Hockley Heath. Across the field you can see two 'needles' pointing skywards: the first, the tall obelisk **F** was erected in 1749 by Thomas Archer of Umberslade to mark his elevation to the peerage; a little further away is a graceful and slender spire of a baptist church **G**, built in 1877.

The countryside seen during the walk is the old heathland of the Forest of Arden. Historically the county is divided into two areas: south of Stratford are the wide landscapes of the Feldon with extensive arable areas; Arden, to the north, is more wooded with sandy and acid soils — farming has always been difficult here and small farmsteads are the norm. There are several fields on the walk where evidence of medieval strip farming will be seen.

ENGLISH WATERSHED

The type of farming is varied — arable fields are not common in the area as they are too small for modern agricultural methods. Cattle can be seen in the well-watered meadows — indeed this area is one of the great watersheds of the land, with some brooks flowing east to the North Sea and others flowing westwards to join the Severn.

Although there is not much sheep farming, dogs should still be kept under control. Many of the farms provide grazing for horses.

The small areas of woodland —

◀ *The topiary garden at Packwood House, believed to date from about 1655, was designed as a horticultural interpretation of the Sermon on the Mount. Its stark symmetry, set among luxurious swathes of lawn, is a remarkable spectacle, providing a stark visual contrast to the meandering lanes (below) that surround it.*

often remnants of the ancient Forest of Arden — provide an extensive environment for wildlife. As there is less pressure on the land for farming, the hedgerows too are microcosms of natural wildlife. If you walk this route in wintertime you will be able to see how much the hedges, now bare, are used for nest building.

All the common birds are present in the area, especially blackbirds, thrushes and magpies. Even the elusive wrens love the cover provided by hedgerows. By the canal there are many pairs of ducks, while Canada geese are now common enough to be a pest to farming.

Rabbits are now numerous and foxes have a good run as this wooded area is not suitable for hunting. The American grey squirrel is present in large numbers — having ousted its indigenous red cousin. (According to local legend the Arden forest was so dense that it was possible for a squirrel to travel the length of the county from tree to tree without ever having to touch the woodland floor.)

Although meadow flowers have largely been eliminated by chemicals there are many varieties of wild flowers along the lanes and the woods are often carpeted with bluebells.

Stratford Canal

This waterway runs for 25½ miles (41 kms) from King's Norton, Birmingham, and through the Warwickshire countryside to the River Avon at Stratford.
It began as a junction with the Worcester and Birmingham Canal in 1793. From the beginning there were financial problems. By the time it reached Hockley Heath three years later all the capital was spent and it was not until 1799 that construction was resumed.

The stretch to Kingswood joining with the Warwick Canal (now the Grand Union) took three more years. Twenty costly locks were necessary and a decade passed before work on the route southwards recommenced. In 1816 Stratford's Bancroft Basin was reached and a connection with the Avon made. Coal was the main cargo south and lime and grain were carried northwards.

Neglect resulted in closure in 1937. However, the National Trust took over the southern section in 1960 and restoration began. In 1964 the Queen Mother reopened the waterway and it is now part of the British Waterways network. Distinctive features include barrel-roofed lock-keepers' cottages, iron splitbridges that make unhitching tow lines unnecessary and five aqueducts — one spanning a valley for ⅓ mile (536 metres).

Lapworth is a canal centre; the Stratford Canal runs parallel with the Grand Union Canal and is host to traditional narrow boats.

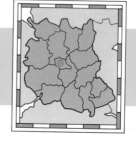
From a Midlands village through pine woods and parkland

This is a gentle walk through woods and parkland deep in the heart of the English countryside. The route includes a visit to the village of Berkswell with its outstanding Norman church **A**.

On leaving the car park you come out by Berkswell's little triangular village green with the old five-holed stocks in the middle. Beyond that is Well House, a red brick building with handsome shaped gables, and in front of it the ancient well which gives the village its name.

A NORMAN CHURCH

The first part of the walk leads through the churchyard, but this church is not a building to rush by, for even a first glance shows how unusual it is. The main structure is sandstone, and has a number of typical Norman round-headed windows. The tower is later, built of different stone, and it has both a clock and a sundial.

The oddest feature, however, is the porch, timber-framed with a priest's room above it. Inside, it is no less remarkable with an unusual wooden font, carved by Robert

J. HARRISON/AQUILA. INSET: M. TWEEDIE/NHPA

▲ The Church of St John the Baptist is one of the finest Norman churches in the Midlands. The buff tip moth (inset) is camouflaged by the buff tip on its wings that resembles a broken twig.

Thompson, who has left his trademark, a tiny carved mouse. It is easy, however, to miss the most interesting feature of all. From the middle of the pews, steps lead down to a beautifully preserved Norman crypt.

The walk goes out into the parkland of Berkswell Hall **B**. The great house looks out across fields and grassland. The centrepiece is the lake, with its tiny island, and the waters are busy with a variety of birds from moorhens to swans and Canada geese. The footpath itself begins on a board walk laid out beside the little stream, then goes into a copse of pine trees. The path is carried over the stream by a rough

plank bridge, but alongside you can see the grander stone bridge built for the path from the house.

The route follows a fine, layered thorn hedge — and it is always a pleasure to see the old rural practices kept up. It then turns in to follow the edge of an extensive pine wood. After the woodland the path turns to cross the fields and a pair of footbridges take it over little streams before it emerges by an extensive

FACT FILE

☀ Berkswell, 6 miles (9 km) west of Coventry

🗺 Pathfinders 955 (SP 27/37) and 935 (SP 28/38), grid reference SP 244791.

miles 0 1 2 3 4 5 6 7 8 9 10 miles
kms 0 1 2 3 4 5 6 7 8 9 10 11 12 13 14 15 kms

◔ Allow 2-3 hours

▭ Very easy walking on paths and over grassland

P Berkswell village car park

🍴 Inn at Berkswell

T Buses from Solihull and Coventry

THE WALK

BERKSWELL

The walk starts at the village car park.

1 Leaving the car park, turn right to the church **A**. Go into the churchyard and follow the footpath sign marked 'Heart of England Way'. Leave the churchyard through the small, wooden gate by the sign Public Footpath. The path now enters the park of Berkswell Hall **B**.

2 Beyond the footbridge at the broad track, turn right following the path by the lake signposted 'Footpath Hampton'. After passing through trees to the next field a wood is ahead on the right. Continue in the same direction along the edge of this wood.

3 Just before reaching the farm buildings on the far side of the wood, you will see a gatepost — but no gate — close to a silage pit. There are two arrows on the post, one of which indicates the path to the right that runs alongside a row of tall thorn trees. The path continues via a series of stiles and footbridges.

4 At the tarmac road, continue straight on through the quarry workings **C** and on through the farmyard of Mercote Mill Farm. Beyond the buildings follow the track round to the right, past the edge of the woodland.

5 At the end of the field, the path swings left towards the road, then right to follow the hedge.

6 At the road turn right.

7 Where the road bends sharply round to the left, continue straight on through the iron gate in the direction indicated by the Public Footpath sign. Head towards the left end of the line of poplars. From there the path goes via stiles to the road.

8 At the road turn right.

9 At the edge of the village before the first of the houses, turn right through a gateway onto the path that is signposted 'Heart of England Way'. This takes you back to the churchyard.

▲*Berkswell Hall and surrounding parkland has records of poaching in 1322. It is now luxury apartments.*

area of quarries **C**. These have become wide scars on the land. This area ends at Mercote Mill Farm.

GAME BIRDS

The walk resumes its now familiar character of fields interspersed with coverts for game birds, before heading towards the road with the old keeper's cottage, and a little wood with a reedy pond in the middle. There is a short section of walking along the country lane past Cornets End farm.

The final part of the walk is by footpath round the edge of the parkland, with a view across to the porticoed front of Berkswell Hall.

▼*A five-holed stock in Berkswell arouses much speculation. A popular theory is a one-legged local offender.*

BOTH PHOTOS J. HARRISON/AQUILA

AQUILA PHOTOGRAPHICS. INSET: MIKE READ/SWIFT PICTURE LIBRARY

▲ *Hampton's five-arched packhorse bridge dates from the 14th century; the railway bridge behind was built in the 19th century. Reeds (inset) line the River Blythe near neighbouring Barston.*

A pleasant country ramble in an ancient royal reserve

Hampton in Arden is less than 3 miles (4.8km) from the small town of Meriden, generally held to be the dead centre of England. This walk explores the countryside of the Forest of Arden, the vast medieval hunting preserve immortalized as a place of sturdy oaks in *As You Like It*. Today, you are more likely to see fields of grain and red-brick villages than patches of woodland.

Hampton is now a dormitory village for the large conurbations of Coventry and Birmingham, but it was a country town until the middle of this century. It has a great

FACT FILE

☀ Hampton in Arden, 3 miles (4.8km) east of Solihull, on the B4102

🗺 Pathfinders 935 (SP 28/38) and 955 (SP 27/37), grid reference SP 205812

miles 0 | 1 | 2 | 3 | 4 | 5 | 6 | 7 | 8 | 9 | 10 miles
kms 0 | 1 | 2 | 3 | 4 | 5 | 6 | 7 | 8 | 9 | 10 | 11 | 12 | 13 | 14 | 15 | kms

◗ Allow 2½ hours

▬ Flat walking on minor roads and field paths. Riverside may be muddy

P Side roads in Hampton

🍺 Pubs in Hampton and Barston

▶ *The Heart Tomb in the chancel of Hampton's church once contained a Knight Templar's heart.*

many charming corners, especially along the High Street, where there are several 17th-century houses, some with jettied upper storeys. Other, later, houses are rendered and decorated with relief plasterwork known as pargetting.

At one end of the High Street is the railway. In the 19th century, Sir Robert Peel lived at the manor house and, as a commissioner of the

AQUILA PHOTOGRAPHICS

THE WALK

HAMPTON IN ARDEN – BARSTON

The starting point of the walk is by the BR station in Hampton in Arden.

1 Turn left along the High Street to the church **A**. Continue south along a cul-de-sac opposite the church. After the road bears right, take a signed path left along a hedged way. Climb a stile into a field, and continue along its left edge to a footbridge over a brook.

2 Cross the brook and continue, crossing a tarmac road and another stream, to join a gravelled drive at Walsal End **B**.

3 Cross a cattle grid by some cottages, and then immediately turn left over another grid. Walk by the converted barn. When the road bears right, keep ahead along a wide grassy track.

4 Where the track bends left, go immediately right over a stile. Go across the middle of the field to a bridge over a brook. Follow the path across another field to a stile. Cross it and follow the hedge on your left to another stile. Follow the track to a road.

5 Turn right, then left at a T-junction into Barston **C**. Follow the road past the church, out of the village, and over the River Blythe **D**. At a junction, go straight ahead down Wootton Lane.

6 Just past Brooklands Farm, cross a stile on your left to take a signed path over rough pasture. Follow the waymarked route across the fields to Bradnock's Marsh Lane.

7 Cross the lane and follow the signed path opposite, keeping the field boundaries to your left and passing a new barn.

8 Where a lane crosses, go straight on over a stile into pastureland. Follow the path ahead with the railway embankment converging on your right. At the embankment, the path meets a track near an old windmill tower.

9 Follow the track over a packhorse bridge **E**. Walk along a raised causeway. Go through a barrier on your left where two paths are indicated. Take the right-hand one, heading towards Hampton church.

10 As the route diverges from the railway embankment, stiles show the line through fields to some houses. The path goes between gardens to come to a cul-de-sac. Turn left, and then over a stile to the right. Follow the signed footpath diagonally across the field to a lane. Turn left to return to Hampton in Arden and the start.

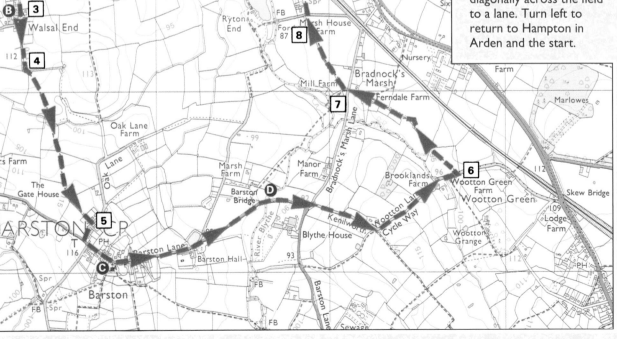

◀Birmingham commuters now dwell in the 16th-century, timber-framed farmhouses in Walsal End and in Barston's thatched cottages (above).

railways, was empowered to ensure that some express trains would stop at the quiet little station.

At the other end of the road, on top of a gentle rise is the church **A**. The tower once had a spire, but this was toppled by a lightning strike in 1643. There is much Norman work in its fabric, and the nave arcade is 700 years old. In the chancel is a Heart Tomb, which once contained the heart of a Knight Templar.

WALSAL END

From Hampton the route takes you south through arable fields, and you come to the hamlet of Walsal End **B**, where the timber-framed buildings that were once the barns and cottages of humble farmers and their

labourers have been converted into elegant and desirable properties.

The route continues through the same gentle countryside. You walk through small fields that are separated by hedgerows, typical of those created in this area up to and including the 19th century.

Some hedges have been grubbed up in recent years in order to make larger tracts of land that are more economical to farm with modern methods, but many of these micro-environments remain to provide homes for small animals, birds and plants. The dog rose, which provides delicate pink flowers in early summer and clusters of shiny scarlet hips in September and October, is particularly abundant.

Less welcome are rabbits, whose numbers have increased to the point where they have become a nuisance to the local farmers, nipping the shoots of growing grain and damaging hedges and other field boundaries. Their only natural control is the foxes that live in the woods and copses and emerge to hunt at night, though you may be lucky and see one on a late summer evening.

AWARD-WINNING VILLAGE

The path through the fields leads to the trim village of Barston **C**, which received an award from Warwickshire County Council for its efforts during the European Conservation Year of 1970. The whole centre of the village, which features many 16th-century cottages, is now a conservation area. The village hall was once a malt barn, and was purchased by the villagers as a

◀Herons and waterfowl can often be seen on shallow, man-made ponds, like this one just beyond the packhorse bridge, created by the damming of the River Blythe in several places along its course.

memorial to those of their number who died in World War I, while the village pub was once a coaching inn.

St Swithin's Church was built in 1721 to replace an earlier building destroyed in a fire. It is unusual for the area, being built of red brick rather than the more common stone.

The village of Barston is sited in a loop of the meandering, reed-edged River Blythe. The lane the route follows out of the village crosses this river via a handsome stone bridge **D**, which was erected by public subscription in 1859.

WILLOW-FRINGED BROOK

The return journey is made along a footpath that follows the valley of the Blythe. The name derives from the Old English word blipe, meaning 'gentle', and this aptly describes the willow-fringed brook, which follows a tortuous course through lush, sometimes boggy meadows. When the fields are flooded in winter, flocks of lapwings descend onto them as they search for insects.

Where the banks of the Blythe are overhung with trees and shrubs, you may sometimes see the shy

In the ponds by the River Blythe, the familiar grey heron stalks prey that swims below the surface of the water.

and elusive kingfisher, the most vividly coloured of all British birds, which dives from perches along the bank to catch small fish. It announces its presence with a flash of metallic blue as it bullets along close to the surface.

In several places, the Blythe has been dammed to create large, shallow millponds on the opposite bank to that along which you are walking. These man-made lakes make ideal hunting grounds for herons, which can often be seen flying over the path, their wings beating ponderously and their legs dangling beneath them. The lakes also attract a variety of waterfowl.

PACKHORSE BRIDGE

The path crosses the river close to Hampton via a weathered, five-arched packhorse bridge **E**. This narrow structure has stood here since the 14th century. On one of its piers is the base of an ancient cross, and the letters H and B, marking the boundary between the two parishes of Hampton and Berkswell. Just ½ mile (0.8km) beyond the bridge, and visible across the meadows, is the tower of Hampton Church, near which the walk ends.

▼*Stiles lead into small fields separated by hedgerows, through countryside little changed since the 19th century.*

The King's Wood

The Forest of Arden may never have been a forest in the sense of a continuous woodland, although one authority claimed at the end of the 19th century that 'even in modern times a squirrel might leap from tree to tree for nearly the whole of Warwickshire'.

'Forests' such as Arden or Sherwood were hunting reserves for the exclusive use of the sovereign. The fact that there were many clearings is evident from the number of places in Arden with the suffix 'ley' (meaning 'open countryside') in their names, such as Henley, Shirley, Honiley and Yardley.

These vast tracts of land — Arden may have stretched from the Severn to the Trent — were protected by strict laws to ensure good sport and adequate cover for game, mainly deer and wild pigs. The undergrowth could not be disturbed, and in some places the gathering of firewood was a serious offence. The penalties for poaching were always severe.

Arden — the name derives from Gaelic and means 'little height' — lay

In the Forest of Arden, old, sturdy oaks like these have been protected by law since before Shakespeare's time.

to the north of the Avon; the rich pastoral lands to the south were known as the Feldon. The first lord of the manor to call himself 'de Eardene' was Radulphus de Hamptone in the reign of King Stephen (1135-1154).

INDEX